THE COLLECTED EDITION OF
THE WORKS OF W. SOMERSET MAUGHAM

THE SUMMING UP

By W. SOMERSET MAUGHAM

LIZA OF LAMBETH
MRS. CRADDOCK
THE MERRY-GO-ROUND
THE EXPLORER
THE MAGICIAN
THE MOON AND SIXPENCE
OF HUMAN BONDAGE
THE TREMBLING OF A LEAF
ON A CHINESE SCREEN
THE PAINTED VEIL
THE CASUARINA TREE
ASHENDEN
THE GENTLEMAN IN THE PARLOUR
CAKES AND ALE
THE FIRST PERSON SINGULAR
THE NARROW CORNER
AH KING
ALTOGETHER (*Collected Short Stories*)
DON FERNANDO
COSMOPOLITANS
THEATRE
THE SUMMING UP
CHRISTMAS HOLIDAY
THE MIXTURE AS BEFORE
BOOKS AND YOU
UP AT THE VILLA
STRICTLY PERSONAL
THE RAZOR'S EDGE
THEN AND NOW
HERE AND THERE (*Collection of Short Stories*)
CREATURES OF CIRCUMSTANCE
CATALINA
QUARTET (*Four Short Stories with Film Scripts*)
TRIO (*Three Short Stories with Film Scripts*)
A WRITER'S NOTEBOOK

The Collected Plays

VOL. 1:   LADY FREDERICK
          MRS. DOT
          JACK STRAW
VOL. 2:   PENELOPE
          SMITH
          THE LAND OF PROMISE
VOL. 3:   OUR BETTERS
          THE UNATTAINABLE
          HOME AND BEAUTY

VOL. 4:   THE CIRCLE
          THE CONSTANT WIFE
          THE BREADWINNER
VOL. 5:   CÆSAR'S WIFE
          EAST OF SUEZ
          THE SACRED FLAME
VOL. 6:   THE UNKNOWN
          FOR SERVICES RENDERED
          SHEPPEY

W. SOMERSET MAUGHAM

THE SUMMING UP

★

WILLIAM HEINEMANN LTD
MELBOURNE :: LONDON :: TORONTO

First published 1938
Collected Edition September 1948
Reprinted 1949, 1951

Printed in France by Régie
LE LIVRE UNIVERSEL, PARIS

I

THIS IS NOT an autobiography nor is it a book of recollections. In one way and another I have used in my writings whatever has happened to me in the course of my life. Sometimes an experience I have had has served as a theme and I have invented a series of incidents to illustrate it; more often I have taken persons with whom I have been slightly or intimately acquainted and used them as the foundation for characters of my invention. Fact and fiction are so intermingled in my work that now, looking back on it, I can hardly distinguish one from the other. It would not interest me to record the facts, even if I could remember them, of which I have already made a better use. They would seem, moreover, very tame. I have had a varied, and often an interesting, life, but not an adventurous one. I have a poor memory. I can never remember a good story till I hear it again and then I forget it before I have had a chance to tell it to somebody else. I have never been able to remember even my own jokes, so that I have been forced to go on making new ones. This disability, I am aware, has made my company less agreeable than it might otherwise have been.

I have never kept a diary. I wish now that during the year that followed my first success as a dramatist I had done so, for I met then many persons of consequence and it might have proved an interesting document. At that period the confidence of the people in the aristocracy and the landed gentry had been shattered by the muddle they had made of things in South Africa, but the aristocracy and the landed gentry had not realized this and they preserved their old self-confidence. At certain political houses I frequented they still talked as though to run the British Empire were their private business. It gave me a peculiar sensation to hear it discussed, when a general election was in the air, whether Tom should have the Home Office and whether Dick would be satisfied with Ireland. I do not suppose that anyone to-day reads the novels of Mrs. Humphry Ward, but dull though they may be, my recollection is that some of them give a very good picture of what the life of the ruling class was then.

Novelists were still much concerned with it and even writers who had never known a lord thought it necessary to write largely about persons of rank. It would astonish anyone who now looked at the playbills of the day to see how many of the characters were titled. Managers thought that they attracted the public, and actors liked to portray them. But as the political importance of the aristocracy dwindled the public took less interest in it. Playgoers began to be ready to observe the actions of people of their own class, the well-to-do merchants and professional men who were then conducting the affairs of the country; and the rule, though never formulated, prevailed that the writer should not introduce persons of title unless they were essential to his theme. It was still impossible to interest the public in the lower classes. Novels and plays that dealt with them were very generally considered sordid. It will be curious to see if now that these classes have acquired political power the public at large will take the same interest in their lives that for so long it took in the lives of the titled, and for a while in those of the opulent bourgeoisie.

During this period I met persons who by their rank, fame or position might very well have thought themselves destined to become historical figures. I did not find them as brilliant as my fancy had painted them. The English are a political nation and I was often asked to houses where politics were the ruling interest. I could not discover in the eminent statesmen I met there any marked capacity. I concluded, perhaps rashly, that no great degree of intelligence was needed to rule a nation. Since then I have known in various countries a good many politicians who have attained high office. I have continued to be puzzled by what seemed to me the mediocrity of their minds. I have found them ill-informed upon the ordinary affairs of life and I have not often discovered in them either subtlety of intellect or liveliness of imagination. At one time I was inclined to think that they owed their illustrious position only to their gift of speech, for it must be next door to impossible to rise to power in a democratic community unless you can catch the ears of the public; and the gift of speech, as we know, is not often accompanied by the power of thought. But since I have seen statesmen who did not seem to me very clever conduct public affairs with reasonable success I cannot but think I was wrong: it must be that to govern a nation you need a specific talent and that this may very well exist without general ability. In the same way I have known men of affairs who have made great fortunes and brought vast enterprises to prosperity, but in everything unconcerned with their business appear to be devoid even of common sense.

Nor was the conversation that I heard then as clever as I had expected. It seldom gave you much to think about. It was easy, though not always gay; amiable and superficial. Serious topics were not dealt with, for there was a feeling that to discuss them in general company was embarrassing, and the fear of 'shop' seemed to prevent people from speaking of the subjects in which they were most interested. So far as I could judge conversation consisted in little more than a decorous badinage; but it was not often that you heard a witticism worth repeating. One might have thought that the only use of culture was to enable one to talk nonsense with distinction. On the whole I think the most interesting and consistently amusing talker I ever knew was Edmund Gosse. He had read a great deal, though not very carefully, it appears, and his conversation was extremely intelligent. He had a prodigious memory, a keen sense of humour, and malice. He had known Swinburne intimately and could talk about him in an entrancing fashion, but he could also talk of Shelley, whom after all he could not possibly have known, as if he had been a bosom-friend. For many years he had been acquainted with eminent persons. I think he was a vain man and he had observed their absurdities with satisfaction. I am sure he made them much more amusing than they really were.

2

I HAVE ALWAYS wondered at the passion many

people have to meet the celebrated. The prestige you acquire by being able to tell your friends that you know famous men proves only that you are yourself of small account. The celebrated develop a technique to deal with the person they come across. They show the world a mask, often an impressive one, but take care to conceal their real selves. They play the part that is expected from them and with practice learn to play it very well, but you are stupid if you think that this public performance of theirs corresponds with the man within.

I have been attached, deeply attached, to a few people; but I have been interested in men in general not for their own sakes, but for the sake of my work. I have not, as Kant enjoined, regarded each man as an end in himself, but as material that might be useful to me as a writer. I have been more concerned with the obscure than with the famous. They are more often themselves. They have had no need to create a figure to protect themselves from the world or to impress it. Their idiosyncrasies have had more chance to develop in the limited circle of their activity, and since they have never been in the public eye it has never occurred to them that they have anything to conceal. They display their oddities because it has never struck them that they are odd. And after all it is with the common run of men that we writers have to deal; kings, dictators, commercial magnates are from our point of view very unsatisfactory. To write about them is a venture that has often tempted writers, but the failure that has attended their efforts shows that such beings are too exceptional to form a proper ground for a work of art. They cannot be made real. The ordinary is the writer's richer field. Its unexpectedness, its singularity, its infinite variety afford unending material. The great man is too often all of a piece; it is the little man that is a bundle of contradictory elements. He is inexhaustible. You never come to the end of the surprises he has in store for you. For my part I would much sooner spend a month on a desert island with a veterinary surgeon than with a prime minister.

3

IN THIS BOOK I am going to try to sort out my thoughts on the subjects that have chiefly interested me during the course of my life. But such conclusions as I have come to have drifted about my mind like the wreckage of a foundered ship on a restless sea. It has seemed to me that if I set them down in some sort of order I should see for myself more distinctly what they really were and so might get some kind of coherence into them. I have long thought I should like to make such an attempt and more than once, when starting on a journey that was to last for several months, have determined to set about it. The opportunity seemed ideal. But I have always found that I was assailed by so many impressions, I saw so many strange things and met so many people who excited my fancy, that I had no time to reflect. The experience of the moment was so vivid that I could not attune my mind to introspection.

I have been held back also by the irksomeness of setting down my thoughts in my own person. For though I have written a good deal from this standpoint I have written as a novelist and so in a manner have been able to regard myself as a character in the story. Long habit has made it more comfortable for me to speak through the creatures of my invention. I can decide what they would think more readily than I can decide what I think myself. The one has always been a pleasure to me; the other has been a labour that I have willingly put off. But now I can afford to put it off no longer. In youth the years stretch before one so long that it is hard to realize that they will ever pass, and even in middle age, with the ordinary expectation of life in these days, it is easy to find excuses for delaying what one would like to do but does not want to; but at last a time comes when death must be considered. Here and there one's contemporaries drop off. We know that all men are mortal (Socrates was a man; therefore—and so forth), but it remains for us little more than a logical premiss till we are forced to recognize that in the ordinary course of things our end can no longer be remote. An occasional glance at the obituary column of The Times has suggested to me that the sixties are very unhealthy; I have long thought that it would exasperate me to die before I had written this book and so it seemed to me that I had better set about it at once. When I have finished it I can face the future with serenity, for I shall have rounded off my life's work. I can no longer persuade myself that I am not ready to write it, since if I have not by now made up my mind about the things that seem of importance to me there is small likelihood that I shall ever do so. I am glad at last to collect all these thoughts that for so long have floated at haphazard on the various levels of my consciousness. When they are written down I shall have finished with them and my mind will be free to occupy itself with other things. For I hope that this will not be the last book I shall write. One does not die immediately one has made one's will; one makes one's will as a precaution. To have settled one's affairs is a very good preparation to leading the rest of one's life without concern for the future. When I have finished this book I shall know where I stand. I can afford then to do what I choose with the years that remain to me.

4

IT IS INEVITABLE that in it I should say many things that I have said before; that is why I have called it The Summing Up. When a judge sums up a case he recapitulates the facts that have been put before the jury and comments on the speeches of counsel. He does not offer new evidence. And since I have put the whole of my life into my books much of what I have to say will naturally have found a place in them. There are few subjects within the compass of my interests that I have not lightly or seriously touched upon. All I can attempt to do now is to give a coherent picture of my feelings and opinions; and here and there, maybe, to state with greater elaboration some idea which the limitations I have thought fit to accept in fiction and in the drama have only allowed me to hint at.

This book must be egotistic. It is about certain subjects that are important to me and it is about myself because I can only treat of these subjects as they have affected me. But it is not about my doings. I have no desire to lay bare my heart, and I put limits to the intimacy that I wish the reader to enter upon with me. There are matters on which I am content to maintain my privacy. No one can tell the whole truth about himself. It is not only vanity that has prevented those who have tried to reveal themselves to the world from telling the whole truth; it is direction of interest; their disappointment with themselves, their surprise that they can do things that seem to them so abnormal, make them place too great an emphasis on occurrences that are more common than they suppose. Rousseau in the course of his Confessions narrates incidents that have profoundly shocked the sensibility of mankind. By describing them so frankly he falsified his values and so gave them in his book a greater importance than they had in his life. They were events among a multitude of others, virtuous or at least neutral, that he omitted because they were too ordinary to seem worth recording. There is a sort of man who pays no attention to his good actions, but is tormented by his bad ones. This is the type that most often writes about himself. He leaves out his redeeming qualities and so appears only weak, unprincipled and vicious.

5

I WRITE this book to disembarrass my soul of certain notions that have hovered about in it too long for my comfort. I do not seek to persuade anybody. I am devoid of the pedagogic instinct and when I know a thing never feel in myself the desire to impart it to others. I do not much care if people agree with me. Of course I think I am right, otherwise I should not think as I do, and they are wrong, but it does not offend me that they should be wrong. Nor does it greatly disturb me to discover that my judgment is at variance with that of the majority. I have a certain confidence in my instinct.

I must write as though I were a person of importance; and indeed, I am—to myself. To myself I am the most important person in the world; though I do not forget that, not even taking into consideration so grand a conception as the Absolute, but from the standpoint of common sense, I am of no consequence whatever. It would have made small difference to the universe if I had never existed. Though I may seem to write as though significance must necessarily be attached to certain of my works, I mean only that they are of moment to me for the purpose of any discussion during which I may have occasion to mention them. I think few serious writers, by which I do not only mean writers of serious things, can be entirely indifferent to the fate that will befall their works after their death. It is pleasant to think, not that one may achieve immortality (immortality for literary productions lasts in any case but a few hundred years and then is seldom more than the immortality of the school-room) but that one may be read with interest by a few generations and find a place, however small, in the history of one's country's literature. But so far as I am concerned, I look upon this modest possibility with scepticism. Even in my life I have seen writers who made much more stir in the world of letters than ever I have, sink into oblivion. When I was young George Meredith and Thomas Hardy seemed certain of survival. They have ceased to mean very much to the youth of to-day. From time to time they will doubtless find a critic in search of a subject to write an article about them, which may cause readers here and there to get out one or other of their books from a library; but I think it is clear that neither of them wrote anything that will be read as Gulliver's Travels, Tristram Shandy or Tom Jones is read.

If in the following pages I seem to express myself dogmatically, it is only because I find it very boring to qualify every phrase with an 'I think' or 'to my mind'. Everything I say is merely an opinion of my own. The

8

reader can take it or leave it. If he has the patience to read what follows he will see that there is only one thing about which I am certain, and this is that there is very little about which one can be certain.

6

WHEN I BEGAN to write I did so as though it were the most natural thing in the world. I took to it as a duck takes to water. I have never quite got over my astonishment at being a writer; there seems no reason for my having become one except an irresistible inclination, and I do not see why such an inclination should have arisen in me. For well over a hundred years my family has practised law. According to the Dictionary of National Biography my grandfather was one of the two founders of the Incorporated Law Society, and in the catalogue of the Library at the British Museum there is a long list of his legal works. He wrote only one book that was not of this character. It was a collection of essays that he had contributed to the solid magazines of the day and he issued it, as became his sense of decorum, anonymously. I once had the book in my hands, a handsome volume bound in calf, but I never read it and I have not been able to get hold of a copy since. I wish I had, for I might have learnt from it something of the kind of man he was. For many years he lived in Chancery Lane, for he became secretary of the Society he had founded, and when he retired to a house in Kensington Gore overlooking the Park, he was presented with a salver, a tea and coffee service and an épergne, in silver, so massive and ornate that they have been ever since an embarrassment to his descendants. An old solicitor, whom I knew when I was a boy, told me that as an articled clerk he was once invited to dine with my grandfather. My grandfather carved the beef and then a servant handed him a dish of potatoes baked in their skins. There are few things better to eat than a potato in its skin, with plenty of butter, pepper and salt, but apparently my grandfather did not think so. He rose in his chair at the head of the table and took the

9

potatoes out of the dish one by one and threw one at each picture on the walls. Then without a word he sat down again and went on with his dinner. I asked my friend what effect this behaviour had on the rest of the company. He told me that no one took any notice. He also told me that my grandfather was the ugliest little man he ever saw. I went once to the building of the Incorporated Society in Chancery Lane to see for myself if he was really so ugly as all that, for there is a portrait of him there. If what my old gentleman said was true the painter must have grossly flattered my grandfather; he has given him very fine dark eyes under black eyebrows, and there is a faintly ironic twinkle in them; a firm jaw, a straight nose and pouting red lips. His dark hair is windswept as becomingly as that of Miss Anita Loos. He is holding a quill and there is a pile of books, doubtless his own, by his side. Notwithstanding his black coat, he does not look so respectable as I should have expected, but slightly mischievous. Many years ago when I was destroying the papers of one of his sons, my uncle, who had died, I came across the diary that my grandfather kept when as a young man at the beginning of the nineteenth century he did what I believe was called the Little Tour, France, Germany and Switzerland; and I remember that when he described the not very impressive fall of the Rhine at Schaffhausen he offered thanks to God Almighty because in creating 'this stupendous cataract' he had given 'His miserable creatures occasion to realize their insignificance in comparison with the prodigious greatness of His works.'

7

MY PARENTS died when I was so young, my mother when I was eight, my father when I was ten, that I know little of them but from hearsay. My father, I do not know why unless he was drawn by some such restlessness for the unknown as has consumed his son, went to Paris and became solicitor to the British Embassy. He had offices just opposite, in the Faubourg St. Honoré, but he lived in what was then called the Avenue d'Antin, a broad street with chestnut trees on each side of it that leads from the Rond Point. He was a great traveller for those days. He had been to Turkey, Greece and Asia Minor and in Morocco as far as Fez, which was a place few people then visited. He had a considerable library of travel books and the apartment in the Avenue d'Antin was filled with the things he had brought back, Tanagra statuettes, Rhodes ware and Turkish daggers in hilts of richly decorated silver. He was forty when he married my mother, who was more than twenty years younger. She was a very beautiful woman and he was a very ugly man. I have been told that they were known in the Paris of that day as Beauty and the Beast. Her father was in the army; he died in India and his widow, my grandmother, after squandering a considerable fortune, settled down in France to live on her pension. She was a woman of character, I suspect, and perhaps of some talent, for she wrote novels in French *pour jeunes filles* and composed the music for drawing-room ballads. I like to think that the novels were read and the ballads sung by Octave Feuillet's high-born heroines. I have a little photograph of her, a middle-aged woman in a crinoline with fine eyes and a look of good-humoured determination. My mother was very small, with large brown eyes and hair of a rich reddish gold, exquisite features and a lovely skin. She was very much admired. One of her great friends was Lady Anglesey, an American woman who died at an advanced age not very long ago, and she told me that she had once said to my mother: 'You're so beautiful and there are so many people in love with you, why are you faithful to that ugly little man you've married?' And my mother answered: 'He never hurts my feelings.'

The only letter of hers I ever saw was one that I came across when I was going through my uncle's papers after his death. He was a clergyman and she asked him to be godfather to one of her sons. She expressed, very simply and piously, the hope that by reason of his holy calling the relationship into which she invited him to enter would have such an influence on the new-born child that he would grow up to be a good, God-fearing man. She was a great novel-reader and in the billiard-room of the apartment in the Avenue d'Antin were two great bookcases filled with Tauchnitz. She suffered from tuberculosis of the lungs and I remember the string of donkeys that stopped at the door to provide her with asses' milk, which at that time was thought to be good for that malady. In the summer we used to take a house at Deauville, not then a fashionable spot, but a little fishing village overshadowed by the smarter Trouville, and towards the end of her life we spent winters at Pau. Once when she was lying in bed, I suppose after a hæmorrhage, and knew she could not live much longer, the thought came to her that her sons when they grew up would not know what she was like when she died, so she called her maid, had herself dressed in an evening gown of white satin and went to the photographer's. She had six sons and died in childbirth. The doctors of the period had a theory that to have a child was beneficial to women suffering from consumption. She was thirty-eight.

After my mother's death, her maid became my nurse. I had till then had French nurses and I had been sent to a French school for children. My knowledge of English must have been slight. I have been told that on one occasion, seeing a horse out of the window of a railway carriage, I cried: '*Regardez, Maman, voilà un 'orse.*'

I think my father had a romantic mind. He took it into his head to build a house to live in during the summer. He bought a piece of land on the top of a hill at Sursenes. The view was splendid over the plain, and in the distance was Paris. There was a road down to the river and by the river lay a little village. It was to be like a villa on the Bosphorus and on the top floor it was surrounded by loggias. I used to go down with him every Sunday by the Seine on a *bateau-mouche* to see how it was getting on. When the roof was on, my father began to furnish it by buying a pair of antique fire-irons. He ordered a great quantity of glass on which he had engraved a sign against the Evil Eye which he had found in Morocco and which the reader may see on the cover of this book. It was a white house and the shutters were painted red. The garden was laid out. The rooms were furnished and then my father died.

8

I HAD BEEN taken away from the French school and went for my lessons every day to the apartment of the English clergyman at the Church attached to the Embassy. His method of teaching me English was to make me read aloud the police-court news in The Standard and I can still remember the horror with which I read the ghastly details of a murder in the train between Paris and Calais. I must then have been nine. I was for long uncertain about the pronunciation of English words and I have never forgotten the roar of laughter that abashed me when in my preparatory school I read out the phrase 'unstable as water' as though unstable rhymed with Dunstable.

I have never had more than two English lessons in my life, for though I wrote essays at school, I do not remember that I ever received any instruction on how to put sentences together. The two lessons I have had were given me so late in life that I am afraid I cannot hope greatly to profit by them. The first was only a few years ago. I was spending some weeks in London and had engaged as temporary secretary a young woman. She was shy, rather pretty, and absorbed in a love affair with a married man. I had written a book called Cakes and Ale and, the typescript arriving one Saturday morning, I asked her if she would be good enough to take it home and correct it over the week-end. I meant her only to make a note of mistakes in spelling that the typist might have made and point out errors occasioned by a handwriting that is not always easy to decipher. But she was a conscientious young person and she took me more literally than I intended. When she brought back the typescript on Monday morning it was accompanied by four foolscap sheets of corrections. I must confess that at the first glance I was a trifle vexed; but then I thought that it would be silly of me not to profit, if I could, by the trouble she had taken and so sat me down to examine them. I suppose the young woman had taken a course at a secretarial college and she had gone through my novel in the same methodical way as her masters had gone through her essays. The remarks that filled the four neat pages of foolscap were incisive and severe. I could not but surmise that the professor of English at the secretarial college did not mince matters. He took a marked line, there could be no doubt about that; and he did not allow that there might be two opinions about anything. His apt pupil would have nothing to do with a preposition at the end of a sentence. A mark of exclamation betokened her disapproval of a colloquial phrase. She had a feeling that you must not use the same word twice on a page and she was ready every time with a synonym to put in its place. If I had indulged myself in the luxury of a sentence of ten lines, she wrote: 'Clarify this. Better break it up into two or more periods.' When I had availed myself of the pleasant pause that is indicated by a semi-colon, she noted: 'A full stop'; and if I had ventured upon a colon she remarked stingingly: 'Obsolete.' But the harshest stroke of all was her comment on what I thought was rather a good joke: 'Are you sure of your facts?' Taking it all in all I am bound to conclude that the professor at her college would not have given me very high marks.

The second lesson I had was given me by a don, both intelligent and charming, who happened to be staying with me when I was myself correcting the typescript of another book. He was good enough to offer to read it. I hesitated, because I knew that he judged from a standpoint of excellence that is hard to attain; and though I was aware that he had a profound knowledge of Elizabethan literature, his inordinate admiration for Esther Waters made me doubtful of his discernment in the productions of our own day: no one could attach so great a value to that work who had an intimate knowledge of the French novel during the nineteenth century. But I was anxious to make my book as good as I could and I hoped to benefit by his criticisms. They were in point of fact lenient. They interested me peculiarly because I inferred that this was the way in which he dealt with the compositions of undergraduates. My don had, I think, a natural gift for language, which it has been his business to cultivate; his taste appeared to me faultless. I was much struck by his insistence on the force of individual words. He liked the stronger word rather than the euphonious. To give an example, I had written that a statue would be placed in a certain square and he suggested that I should write: the statue will stand. I had not done that because my ear was offended by the alliteration. I noticed also that he had a feeling that words should be used not only to balance a sentence but to balance an idea. This is sound, for an idea may lose its effect if it is delivered abruptly; but it is a matter of delicacy, since it may well lead to verbiage. Here a knowledge of stage dialogue should help. An actor will sometimes say to an author: 'Couldn't you give me a word or two more in this speech? It seems to take away all the point of my line if I have nothing else to say.' As I listened to my don's remarks I could not but think how much better I should write now if in my youth I had had the advantage of such sensible, broad-minded and kindly advice.

9

AS IT IS, I have had to teach myself. I have looked at the stories I wrote when I was very young in order to discover what natural aptitude I had, my original stock-in-trade, before I developed it by taking thought. The manner had a superciliousness that perhaps my years excused and an irascibility that was a defect of nature; but I am speaking now only of the way in which I expressed myself. It seems to me that I had a natural lucidity and a knack for writing easy dialogue.

When Henry Arthur Jones, then a well-known playwright, read my first novel, he told a friend that in due course I should be one of the most successful dramatists of the day. I suppose he saw in it directness and an effective way of presenting a scene that suggested a sense of the theatre. My language was commonplace, my vocabulary limited, my grammar shaky and my phrases hackneyed. But to write was an instinct that seemed as natural to me as to breathe, and I did not stop to consider if I wrote well or badly. It was not till some years later that it dawned upon me that it was a delicate art that must be painfully acquired. The discovery was forced upon me by the difficulty I found in getting my meaning down on paper. I wrote dialogue fluently, but when it came to a page of description I found myself entangled in all sorts of quandaries. I would struggle for a couple of hours over two or three sentences that I could in no way manage to straighten out. I made up my mind to teach myself how to write. Unfortunately I had no one to help me. I made many mistakes. If I had had someone to guide me like the charming don of whom I spoke just now I might have been saved much time. Such a one might have told me that such gifts as I had lay in one direction and that they must be cultivated in that direction; it was useless to try to do something for which I had no aptitude. But at that time a florid prose was admired. Richness of texture was sought by means of a jewelled phrase and sentences stiff with exotic epithets: the ideal was a brocade so heavy with gold that it stood up by itself. The intelligent young read Walter Pater with enthusiasm. My common sense suggested to me that it was anæmic stuff; behind those elaborate, gracious periods I was conscious of a tired, wan personality. I was young, lusty and energetic; I wanted fresh air, action, violence, and I found it hard to breathe that dead, heavily-scented atmosphere and sit in those hushed rooms in which it was indecorous to speak above a whisper. But I would not listen to my common sense. I persuaded myself that this was the height of culture and turned a scornful shoulder to the outside world where men shouted and swore, played the fool, wenched and got drunk. I read Intentions and The Picture of Dorian Gray. I was intoxicated by the colour and rareness of the fantastic words that thickly stud the pages of Salome. Shocked by the poverty of my own vocabulary, I went to the British Museum with pencil and paper and noted down the names of curious jewels, the Byzantine hues of old enamels, the sensual feel of textiles, and made elaborate sentences to bring them in. Fortunately I could never find an opportunity to use them and they lie there yet in an old note-book ready for anyone who has a mind to write nonsense. It was generally thought then that the Authorized Version of the Bible was the greatest piece of prose that the English language has produced. I read it diligently, especially the Song of Solomon, jotting down for future use turns of phrase that struck me and making lists of unusual or beautiful words. I studied Jeremy Taylor's Holy Dying. In order to assimilate his style I copied out passages and then tried to write them down from memory.

The first fruit of this labour was a little book about Andalusia called The Land of the Blessed Virgin. I had occasion to read parts of it the other day. I know Andalusia a great deal better than I knew it then, and I have changed my mind about a good many things of which I wrote. Since it has continued in America to have a small sale it occurred to me that it might be worth while to revise it. I soon saw that this was impossible. The book was written by someone I have completely forgotten. It bored me to distraction. But what I am concerned with is the prose, for it was as an exercise in style that I wrote it. It is wistful, allusive and elaborate. It has neither case nor spontaneity. It smells of hot-house plants and Sunday dinner like the air in the greenhouse that leads out of the dining-room of a big house in Bayswater. There are a great many melodious adjectives. The vocabulary is sentimental. It does not remind one of an Italian brocade, with its rich pattern of gold, but of a curtain material designed by Burne-Jones and reproduced by Morris.

10

I DO NOT know whether it was a subconscious feeling that this sort of writing was contrary to my bent or a naturally methodical cast of mind that led me then to turn my attention to the writers of the Augustan Period. The prose of Swift enchanted me. I made up my mind that this was the perfect way to write and I started to work on him in the same way as I had done with Jeremy Taylor. I chose The Tale of a Tub. It is said that when the Dean re-read it in his old age he cried: 'What genius I had then!' To my mind his genius was better shown in other works. It is a tiresome allegory and the irony is facile. But the style is admirable. I cannot imagine that English can be better written. Here are no flowery periods, fantastic turns of phrase or high-flown images. It is a civilized prose, natural, discreet and pointed. There is no attempt to surprise by an extravagant vocabulary. It looks as though Swift made do with the first word that came to hand, but since he had an acute and logical brain it was always the right one, and he put it in the right place. The strength and balance of his sentences are due to an exquisite taste. As I had done before I copied passages and then tried to write them out again from memory. I tried altering words or the order in which they were set. I found that the only possible words were those Swift had used and that the order in which he had placed them was the only possible order. It is an impeccable prose.

But perfection has one grave defect: it is apt to be dull. Swift's prose is like a French canal, bordered with poplars, that runs through a gracious and undulating country. Its tranquil charm fills you with satisfaction, but it neither excites the emotions nor stimulates the imagination. You go on and on and presently you are a trifle bored. So, much as you may admire Swift's wonderful lucidity, his terseness, his naturalness, his lack of affectation, you find your attention wandering after a while unless his matter peculiarly interests you. I think if I had my time over again I would give to the prose of Dryden the close study I gave to that of Swift. I did not come across it till I had lost the inclination to take so much pains. The prose of Dryden is delicious. It has not the perfection of Swift nor the easy elegance of Addison, but it has a springtime gaiety, a conversational ease, a blithe spontaneousness that are enchanting.

Dryden was a very good poet, but it is not the general opinion that he had a lyrical quality; it is strange that it is just this that sings in his softly sparkling prose. Prose had never been written in England like that before; it has seldom been written like that since. Dryden flourished at a happy moment. He had in his bones the sonorous periods and the baroque massiveness of Jacobean language and under the influence of the nimble and well-bred felicity that he learnt from the French he turned it into an instrument that was fit not only for solemn themes but also to express the light thought of the passing moment. He was the first of the rococo artists. If Swift reminds you of a French canal, Dryden recalls an English river winding its cheerful way round hills, through quietly busy towns and by nestling villages, pausing now in a noble reach and then running powerfully through a woodland country. It is alive, varied, windswept; and it has the pleasant open-air smell of England.

The work I did was certainly very good for me. I began to write better; I did not write well. I wrote stiffly and self-consciously. I tried to get a pattern into my sentences, but did not see that the pattern was evident. I took care how I placed my words, but did not reflect that an order that was natural at the beginning of the eighteenth century was most unnatural at the beginning of ours. My attempt to write in the manner of Swift made it impossible for me to achieve the effect of inevitable rightness that was just what I so much admired in him. I then wrote a number of plays and ceased to occupy myself with anything but dialogue. It was not till five years had passed that I set out again to write a novel. By then I no longer had any ambition to be a stylist; I put aside all thought of fine writing. I wanted to write without any frills of language, in as bare and unaffected a manner as I could. I had so much to say that I could afford to waste no words. I wanted merely to set down the facts. I began with the impossible aim of using no adjectives at all. I thought that if you could find the exact term a qualifying epithet could be dispensed with. As I saw it in my mind's eye my book would have the appearance of an immensely long telegram in which for economy's sake you had left out every word that was not necessary to make the sense clear. I have not read it since I corrected the proofs and do not know how near I came to doing what I tried. My impression is that it is written at least more naturally than anything I had written before; but I am sure that it is often slipshod and I daresay there are in it a good many mistakes in grammar.

Since then I have written many other books; and though ceasing my methodical study of the old masters (for though the spirit is willing, the flesh is weak), I have continued with increasing assiduity to try to write better. I discovered my limitations and it seemed to me that the only sensible thing was to aim at what excellence I could within them. I knew that I had no lyrical quality. I had a small vocabulary and no efforts that I could make to enlarge it much availed me. I had little gift of metaphor; the original and striking simile seldom occurred to me. Poetic flights and the great imaginative sweep were beyond my powers. I could admire them in others as I could admire their far-fetched tropes and the unusual but suggestive language in which they clothed their thoughts but my own invention never presented me with such embellishments; and I was tired of trying to do what did not come easily to me. On the other hand, I had an acute power of observation and it seemed to me that I could see a great many things that other people missed. I could put down in clear terms what I saw. I had a logical sense, and if no great feeling for the richness and strangeness of words, at all events a lively appreciation of their sound. I knew that I should never write as well as I could wish, but I thought with pains I could arrive at writing as well as my natural defects allowed. On taking thought it seemed to me that I must aim at lucidity, simplicity and euphony. I have put these three qualities in the order of the importance I assigned to them.

II

I HAVE NEVER had much patience with the writers

who claim from the reader an effort to understand their meaning. You have only to go to the great philosophers to see that it is possible to express with lucidity the most subtle reflections. You may find it difficult to understand the thought of Hume, and if you have no philosophical training its implications will doubtless escape you; but no one with any education at all can fail to understand exactly what the meaning of each sentence is. Few people have written English with more grace than Berkeley. There are two sorts of obscurity that you find in writers. One is due to negligence and the other to wilfulness. People often write obscurely because they have never taken the trouble to learn to write clearly. This sort of obscurity you find too often in modern philosophers, in men of science, and even in literary critics. Here it is indeed strange. You would have thought that men who passed their lives in the study of the great masters of literature would be sufficiently sensitive to the beauty of language to write if not beautifully at least with perspicuity. Yet you will find in their works sentence after sentence that you must read twice to discover the sense. Often you can only guess at it, for the writers have evidently not said what they intended.

Another cause of obscurity is that the writer is himself not quite sure of his meaning. He has a vague impression of what he wants to say, but has not, either from lack of mental power or from laziness, exactly formulated it in his mind and it is natural enough that he should not find a precise expression for a confused idea. This is due largely to the fact that many writers think, not before, but as they write. The pen originates the thought. The disadvantage of this, and indeed it is a danger against which the author must be always on his guard, is that there is a sort of magic in the written word. The idea acquires substance by taking on a visible nature, and then stands in the way of its own clarification. But this sort of obscurity merges very easily into the wilful. Some writers who do not think clearly are inclined to suppose that their thoughts have a significance greater than at first sight appears. It is flattering to believe that they are too profound to be expressed so clearly that all who run may read, and very naturally it does not occur to such writers that the fault is with their own minds which have not the faculty of precise reflection. Here again the magic of the written word obtains. It is very easy to persuade oneself that a phrase that one does not quite understand may mean a great deal more than one realizes. From this there is only a little way to go to fall into the habit of setting down one's impressions in all their original vagueness. Fools can always be found to discover a hidden sense in them. There is another form of wilful obscurity that masquerades as aristocratic exclusiveness. The author wraps his meaning in mystery so that the vulgar shall not participate in it. His soul is a secret garden into which the elect may penetrate only after overcoming a number of perilous obstacles. But this kind of obscurity is not only pretentious; it is short-sighted. For time plays it an odd trick. If the sense is meagre time reduces it to a meaningless verbiage that no one thinks of reading. This is the fate that has befallen the lucubrations of those French writers who were seduced by the example of Guillaume Apollinaire. But occasionally it throws a sharp cold light on what had seemed profound and thus discloses the fact that these contortions of language disguised very commonplace notions. There are few of Mallarmé's poems now that are not clear; one cannot fail to notice that his thought singularly lacked originality. Some of his phrases were beautiful; the materials of his verse were the poetic platitudes of his day.

12

SIMPLICITY IS not such an obvious merit as lucidity. I have aimed at it because I have no gift for richness. Within limits I admire richness in others, though I find it difficult to digest in quantity. I can read one page of Ruskin with delight, but twenty only with weariness. The rolling period, the stately epithet, the noun rich in poetic associations, the subordinate clauses that give the sentence weight and magnificence, the grandeur like that of wave following wave in the open sea; there is no doubt that in all this there is something inspiring. Words thus strung together fall on the ear like music. The appeal is sensuous rather than intellectual, and the beauty of the sound leads you easily to conclude that you need not bother about the meaning. But words are tyrannical things, they exist for their meanings, and if you will not pay attention to these, you cannot pay attention at all. Your mind wanders. This kind of writing demands a subject that will suit it. It is surely out of place to write in the grand style of inconsiderable things. No one wrote in this manner with greater success than Sir Thomas Browne, but even he did not always escape this pitfall. In the last chapter of Hydriotaphia the matter, which is the destiny of man, wonderfully fits the baroque splendour of the language, and here the Norwich doctor produced a piece of prose that has never been surpassed in our literature; but when he describes the finding of his urns in the same splendid manner the effect (at least to my taste) is less happy. When a modern writer is grandiloquent to tell you whether or no a little trollop shall hop into bed with a commonplace young man you are right to be disgusted.

But if richness needs gifts with which everyone is not endowed, simplicity by no means comes by nature. To achieve it needs rigid discipline. So far as I know ours is the only language in which it has been found necessary to give a name to the piece of prose which is described as the purple patch; it would not have been necessary to do so unless it were characteristic. English prose is elaborate rather than simple. It was not always so. Nothing could be more racy, straightforward and alive than the prose of Shakespeare; but it must be remembered that this was dialogue written to be spoken. We do not know how he would have written if like Corneille he had composed prefaces to his plays. It may be that they would have been as euphuistic as the letters of Queen Elizabeth. But earlier prose, the prose of Sir Thomas More, for instance, is neither ponderous, flowery nor oratorical. It smacks of the English soil. To my mind King James's Bible has been a very harmful influence on English prose. I am not so stupid as to deny its great beauty. It is majestical. But the Bible is an oriental book. Its alien imagery has nothing to do with us. Those hyperboles, those luscious metaphors, are foreign to our genius. I cannot but think that not the least of the misfortunes that the Secession from Rome brought upon the spiritual life of our country is that this work for so long a period became the daily, and with many the only, reading of our people. Those rhythms, that powerful vocabulary, that grandiloquence, became part and parcel of the national sensibility. The plain, honest English speech was over-whelmed with ornament. Blunt Englishmen twisted their tongues to speak like Hebrew prophets. There was evidently something in the English temper to which this was congenial, perhaps a native lack of precision in thought, perhaps a naïve delight in fine words for their own sake, an innate eccentricity and love of embroidery, I do not know; but the fact remains that ever since, English prose has had to struggle against the tendency to luxuriance. When from time to time the spirit of the language has reasserted itself, as it did with Dryden and the writers of Queen Anne, it was only to be submerged once more by the pomposities of Gibbon and Dr. Johnson. When English prose recovered simplicity with Hazlitt, the Shelley of the letters and Charles Lamb at his best, it lost it again with de Quincey, Carlyle, Meredith and Walter Pater. It is obvious that the grand style is more striking than the plain. Indeed many people think that a style that does not attract notice is not style. They will admire Walter Pater's, but will read an essay by Matthew Arnold without giving a moment's attention to the elegance, distinction and sobriety with which he set down what he had to say.

The dictum that the style is the man is well known. It is one of those aphorisms that say too much to mean a great deal. Where is the man in Goethe, in his bird-like lyrics or in his clumsy prose? And Hazlitt? But I suppose that if a man has a confused mind he will write in a confused way, if his temper is capricious his prose will be fantastical, and if he has a quick, darting intelligence that is reminded by the matter in hand of a hundred things he will, unless he has great self-control, load his pages with metaphor and simile. There is a great difference between the magniloquence of the Jacobean writers, who were intoxicated with the new wealth that had lately been brought into the language, and the turgidity of Gibbon and Dr. Johnson, who were the victims of bad theories. I can read every word that Dr. Johnson wrote with delight, for he had good sense, charm and wit. No one could have written better if he had not wilfully set himself to write in the grand style. He knew good English when he saw it. No critic has praised Dryden's prose more aptly. He said of him that he appeared to have no art other than that of expressing with clearness what he thought with vigour. And one of his Lives he finished with the words: 'Whoever wishes to attain an English style, familiar but not coarse, and elegant but not ostentatious, must give his days and nights to the volumes of Addison.' But when he himself sat down to write it was with a very different aim. He mistook the orotund for the dignified. He had not the good breeding to see that simplicity and naturalness are the truest mark of distinction.

For to write good prose is an affair of good manners. It is, unlike verse, a civil art. Poetry is baroque. Baroque is tragic, massive and mystical. It is elemental. It demands depth and insight. I cannot but feel that the prose writers of the baroque period, the authors of King James's Bible, Sir Thomas Browne, Glanville, were poets who had lost their way. Prose is a rococo art. It needs taste rather than power, decorum rather than inspiration and vigour rather than grandeur. Form for the poet is the bit and the bridle without which (unless you are an acrobat) you cannot ride your horse; but for the writer of prose it is the chassis without which your car does not exist. It is not an accident that the best prose was written when rococo, with its elegance and moderation, at its birth attained its greatest excellence. For rococo was evolved when

25

baroque had become declamatory and the world, tired of the stupendous, asked for restraint. It was the natural expression of persons who valued a civilized life. Humour, tolerance and horse-sense made the great tragic issues that had preoccupied the first half of the seventeenth century seem excessive. The world was a more comfortable place to live in and perhaps for the first time in centuries the cultivated classes could sit back and enjoy their leisure. It has been said that good prose should resemble the conversation of a well-bred man. Conversation is only possible when men's minds are free from pressing anxieties. Their lives must be reasonably secure and they must have no grave concern about their souls. They must attach importance to the refinements of civilisation. They must value courtesy, they must pay attention to their persons (and have we not also been told that good prose should be like the clothes of a well-dressed man, appropriate but unobtrusive?), they must fear to bore, they must be neither flippant nor solemn, but always apt; and they must look upon 'enthusiasm' with a critical glance. This is a soil very suitable for prose. It is not to be wondered at that it gave a fitting opportunity for the appearance of the best writer of prose that our modern world has seen, Voltaire. The writers of English, perhaps owing to the poetic nature of the language, have seldom reached the excellence that seems to have come so naturally to him. It is in so far as they have approached the ease, sobriety and precision of the great French masters that they are admirable.

13

WHETHER YOU ascribe importance to euphony, the last of the three characteristics that I mentioned, must depend on the sensitiveness of your ear. A great many readers, and many admirable writers, are devoid of this quality. Poets as we know have always made a great use of alliteration. They are persuaded that the repetition of a sound gives an effect of beauty. I do not think it does so in prose. It seems to me that in prose alliteration should be used only for a special reason; when used by accident it falls on the ear very disagreeably. But its accidental use is so common that one can only suppose that the sound of it is not universally offensive. Many writers without distress will put two rhyming words together, join a monstrous long adjective to a monstrous long noun, or between the end of one word and the beginning of another have a conjunction of consonants that almost breaks your jaw. These are trivial and obvious instances. I mention them only to prove that if careful writers can do such things it is only because they have no ear. Words have weight, sound and appearance; it is only by considering these that you can write a sentence that is good to look at and good to listen to.

I have read many books on English prose, but have found it hard to profit by them; for the most part they are vague, unduly theoretical, and often scolding. But you cannot say this of Fowler's Dictionary of English Usage. It is a valuable work. I do not think anyone writes so well that he cannot learn much from it. It is lively reading. Fowler liked simplicity, straightforwardness and common sense. He had no patience with pretentiousness. He had a sound feeling that idiom was the backbone of a language and he was all for the racy phrase. He was no slavish admirer of logic and was willing enough to give usage right of way through the exact demesnes of grammar. English grammar is very difficult and few writers have avoided making mistakes in it. So heedful a writer as Henry James, for instance, on occasion wrote so ungrammatically that a schoolmaster, finding such errors in a schoolboy's essay, would be justly indignant. It is necessary to know grammar, and it is better to write grammatically than not, but it is well to remember that grammar is common speech formulated. Usage is the only test. I would prefer a phrase that was easy and unaffected to a phrase that was grammatical. One of the differences between French and English is that in French you can be grammatical with complete naturalness, but in English not invariably. It is a difficulty in writing English that the sound of the living voice dominates the look of the printed word. I have given the matter of style a great deal of thought and have taken great pains. I have written few pages that I feel I could not improve and far too many that I have left with dissatisfaction because, try as I would, I could do no better. I cannot say of myself what Johnson said of Pope: 'He never passed a fault unamended by indifference, nor quitted it by despair.' I do not write as I want to; I write as I can.

But Fowler had no ear. He did not see that simplicity may sometimes make concessions to euphony. I do not think a far-fetched, an archaic or even an affected word is out of place when it sounds better than the blunt, obvious one or when it gives a sentence a better balance. But, I hasten to add, though I think you may without misgiving make this concession to pleasant sound, I think you should make none to what may obscure your meaning. Anything is better than not to write clearly. There is nothing to be said against lucidity, and against simplicity only the possibility of dryness. This is a risk that is well worth taking when you reflect how much better it is to be bald than to wear a curly wig. But there is in euphony a danger that must be considered. It is very likely to be monotonous. When George Moore began to write, his style was poor; it gave you the impression that he wrote on wrapping paper with a blunt pencil. But he developed gradually a very musical English. He learnt to write sentences that fall away on the ear with a misty languor and it delighted him so much that he could never have enough of it. He did not escape monotony. It is like the sound of water lapping a shingly beach, so soothing that you presently cease to be sensible of it. It is so mellifluous that you hanker for some harshness, for an abrupt dissonance, that will interrupt the silky concord. I do not know how one can guard against this. I suppose the best chance is to have a more lively faculty of boredom than one's readers so that one is wearied before they are. One must always be on the watch for mannerisms and when certain cadences come too easily to the pen ask oneself whether they have not become mechanical. It is very hard to discover the exact point where the idiom one has formed to express oneself has lost its tang. As Dr. Johnson said: 'He that has once studiously formed a style, rarely writes afterwards with complete ease'. Admirably as I think Matthew Arnold's style was suited to his particular purposes, I must admit that his mannerisms are often irritating. His style was an instrument that he had forged once for all; it was not like the human hand capable of performing a variety of actions.

If you could write lucidly, simply, euphoniously and yet with liveliness you would write perfectly: you would write like Voltaire. And yet we know how fatal the pursuit of liveliness may be: it may result in the tiresome acrobatics of Meredith. Macaulay and Carlyle were in their different ways arresting; but at the heavy cost of naturalness. Their flashy effects distract the mind. They destroy their persuasiveness; you would not believe a man was very intent on ploughing a furrow if he carried a hoop with him and jumped through it at every other step. A good style should show no sign of effort. What is written should seem a happy accident. I think no one in France now writes more admirably than Colette, and such is the ease of her expression that you cannot bring yourself to believe that she takes any trouble over it. I am told that there are pianists who have a natural technique so that they can play in a manner that most executants can achieve only as the result of unremitting toil, and I am willing to believe that there are writers who are equally fortunate. Among them I was much inclined to place Colette. I asked her. I was exceedingly surprised to hear that she wrote everything over and over again. She told me that she would often spend a whole morning working upon a single page. But it does not matter how one gets the effect of ease. For my part, if I get it at all, it is only by strenuous effort. Nature seldom provides me with the word, the turn of phrase, that is appropriate without being far-fetched or commonplace.

14

I HAVE read that Anatole France tried to use only the constructions and the vocabulary of the writers of the seventeenth century whom he so greatly admired. I do not know if it is true. If so, it may explain why there is some lack of vitality in his beautiful and simple French. But simplicity is false when you do not say a thing that you should say because you cannot say it in a certain way. One should write in the manner of one's period. The language is alive and constantly changing; to try to write like the authors of a distant past can only give rise to artificiality. I should not hesitate to use the common phrases of the day, knowing that their vogue was ephemeral, or slang, though aware that in ten years it might be incomprehensible, if they gave vividness and actuality. If the style has a classical form it can support the discreet use of a phraseology that has only a local and temporary aptness. I would sooner a writer were vulgar than mincing; for life is vulgar, and it is life he seeks.

I think that we English authors have much to learn from our fellow authors in America. For American writing has escaped the tyranny of King James's Bible and American writers have been less affected by the old masters whose mode of writing is part of our culture. They have formed their style, unconsciously perhaps, more directly from the living speech that surrounds them; and at its best it has a directness, a vitality and a drive that give our more urbane manner an air of languor. It has been an advantage to American writers, many of whom at one time or another have been reporters, that their journalism has been written in a more trenchant, nervous, graphic English than ours. For we read the newspaper now as our ancestors read the Bible. Not without profit either; for the newspaper, especially when it is of the popular sort, offers us a part of experience that we writers cannot afford to miss. It is raw material straight from the knacker's yard, and we are stupid if we turn up our noses because it smells of blood and sweat. We cannot, however willingly we would, escape the influence of this work-aday prose. But the journalism of a period has very much the same style; it might all have been written by the same hand; it is impersonal. It is well to counteract its effect by reading of another kind. One can do this only by keeping constantly in touch with the writing of an age not too remote from one's own. So can one have a standard by which to test one's own style and an ideal which in one's modern way one can aim at. For my part the two writers I have found most useful to study for this purpose are Hazlitt and Cardinal Newman. I would try to imitate neither. Hazlitt can be unduly rhetorical; and sometimes his decoration is as fussy as Victorian Gothic. Newman can be a trifle flowery. But at their best both are admirable. Time has little touched their style; it is almost contemporary. Hazlitt is vivid, bracing and energetic; he has strength and liveliness. You feel the man in his phrases, not the mean, querulous, disagreeable man that he appeared to the world that knew him, but the man within of his own ideal vision. (And the man within us is as true in reality as the man, pitiful and halting, of our outward seeming.) Newman had an exquisite grace, music, playful sometimes and sometimes grave, a woodland beauty of phrase, dignity and mellowness. Both wrote with extreme lucidity. Neither is quite as simple as the purest taste demands. Here I think Matthew Arnold excels them. Both had a wonderful balance of phrase and both knew how to write sentences pleasing to the eye. Both had an ear of extreme sensitiveness.

If anyone could combine their merits in the manner of writing of the present day he would write as well as it is possible for anyone to write.

15

FROM time to time I have asked myself whether I should have been a better writer if I had devoted my whole life to literature. Somewhat early, but at what age I cannot remember, I made up my mind that, having but one life, I should like to get the most I could out of it. It did not seem to me enough merely to write. I wanted to make a pattern of my life, in which writing would be an essential element, but which would include all the other activities proper to man, and which death would in the end round off in complete fulfilment. I had many disabilities. I was small; I had endurance but little physical strength; I stammered; I was shy; I had poor health. I had no facility for games, which play so great a part in the normal life of Englishmen; and I had, whether for any of these reasons or from nature I do not know, an instinctive shrinking from my fellow men that has made it difficult for me to enter into any familiarity with them. I have loved individuals; I have never much cared for men in the mass. I have none of that engaging come-hitherness that makes people take to one another on first acquaintance. Though in the course of years I have learnt to assume an air of heartiness when forced into contact with a stranger, I have never liked anyone at first sight. I do not think I have ever addressed someone I did not know in a railway carriage or spoken to a fellow-passenger on board ship unless he first spoke to me. The weakness of my flesh has prevented me from enjoying that communion with the human race that is engendered by alcohol; long before I could reach the state of intoxication that enables so many, more happily constituted, to look upon all men as their brothers, my stomach has turned upon me and I have been as sick as a dog. These are grave disadvantages both to the writer and the man. I have had to make the best of them. I have followed the pattern I made with persistence. I do not claim that it was a perfect one. I think it was the best that I could hope for in the circumstances and with the very limited powers that were granted to me by nature.

Looking for the special function of man Aristotle decided that since he shares growth with the plants and perception with the beasts, and alone has a rational element, his function is the activity of the soul. From this he concluded, not as you would have thought sensible that man should cultivate the three forms of activity which he ascribed to him, but that he should pursue only that which is especial to him. Philosophers and moralists have looked at the body with misgiving. They have pointed out that its satisfactions are brief. But a pleasure is none the less a pleasure because it does not please for ever. It is delightful to plunge into cold water on a hot day even though in a moment your skin is no longer sensitive to the coldness. White is no whiter if it lasts for a year or a day. I looked upon it then as part of the pattern I was attempting to draw to experience all the pleasures of sense. I have not been afraid of excess: excess on occasion is exhilarating. It prevents moderation from acquiring the deadening effect of a habit. It tonifies the system and rests the nerves. The spirit is often most free when the body is satiated with pleasure; indeed, sometimes the stars shine more brightly seen from the gutter than from the hilltop. The keenest pleasure to which the body is susceptible is that of sexual congress. I have known men who gave up their whole lives to this; they are grown old now, but I have noticed, not without surprise, that they look upon them as well spent. It has been my misfortune that a native fastidiousness has prevented me from indulging as much in this particular delight as I might have. I have exercised moderation because I was hard to please. When from time to time I have seen the persons with whom the great lovers satisfied their desires I have been more often astonished by the robustness of their appetites than envious of their successes. It is obvious that you need not often go hungry if you are willing to dine off mutton hash and turnip tops.

Most people live haphazard lives subject to the varying winds of fortune. Many are forced by the situation in which they were born and the necessity of earning a living to keep to a straight and narrow road in which there is no possibility of turning to the right or to the left. Upon these the pattern is imposed. Life itself has forced it on them. There is no reason why such a pattern should not be as complete as that which anyone has tried self-consciously to make. But the artist is in a privileged position. I use the word artist, not meaning to attach any measure of value to what he produces, but merely to signify someone who is occupied with the arts. I wish I could find a better word. Creator is pretentious and seems to make a claim to originality that can seldom be justified. Craftsman is not enough. A carpenter is a craftsman, and though he may be in the narrower sense an artist, he has not as a rule the freedom of action which the most incompetent scribbler, the poorest dauber, possesses. The artist can within certain limits make what he likes of his life. In other callings, in medicine for instance or the law, you are free to choose whether you will adopt them or not, but having chosen, you are free no longer. You are bound by the rules of your profession; a standard of conduct is imposed upon you. The pattern is predetermined. It is only the artist, and maybe the criminal, who can make his own.

Perhaps it was a natural sense of tidiness that engaged me, when still so young, to design a pattern for my life; perhaps it was due to something I discovered in myself about which I shall have a little to say later. The defect of such an undertaking is that it may kill spontaneity. One great difference between the persons of real life and the persons of fiction is that the persons of real life are creatures of impulse. It has been said that metaphysics is the finding of bad reasons for what we believe upon instinct; and it might be said also that in the conduct of life we make use of deliberation to justify ourselves in doing what we want to do. And to surrender to impulse is part of the pattern. I think a greater defect is that it leads you to live too much in the future. I have long known that this was a fault of mine and have in vain tried to correct it. I have never, except by an effort of will, wished that the passing moment might linger so that I could get more enjoyment from it, for even when it has brought me something I had immensely looked forward to, my imagination in the very moment of fulfilment has been busy with the problematical delight of whatever was to come. I have never walked down the south side of Piccadilly without being all in a dither about what was happening on the north. This is folly. The passing moment is all we can be sure of; it is only common sense

34

to extract its utmost value from it; the future will one day be the present and will seem as unimportant as the present does now. But common sense avails me little. I do not find the present unsatisfactory; I merely take it for granted. It is interwoven in the pattern and what interests me is what remains to come.

I have made a great many mistakes. I have at times fallen victim to a snare to which the writer is peculiarly liable, the desire to carry out in my own life certain actions which I made the characters of my invention do. I have attempted things that were foreign to my nature and obstinately persevered in them because in my vanity I would not confess myself beaten. I have paid too much attention to the opinion of others. I have made sacrifices to unworthy objects because I had not the courage to inflict pain. I have committed follies. I have a sensitive conscience, and I have done certain things in my life that I am unable entirely to forget; if I had been fortunate enough to be a Catholic I could have delivered myself of them at confession and after performing the penance imposed received absolution and put them out of my mind for ever. I have had to deal with them as my common sense suggested. I do not regret them, for I think it is because of my own grave faults that I have learnt indulgence to others. It took me a long time. In youth I was harshly intolerant. I remember my indignation upon hearing someone make the remark, not an original one, but new to me then, that hypocrisy was the tribute that vice paid to virtue. I thought that one should have the courage of one's vices. I had ideals of honesty, uprightness, truth; I was impatient not of human weakness, but of cowardice, and I would make no allowances for those who hedged and temporized. It never occurred to me that no one stood in greater need of indulgence than I.

16

AT FIRST sight it is curious that our own offences should seem to us so much less heinous than the offences of others. I suppose the reason is that we know all the circumstances that have occasioned them and so manage to excuse in ourselves what we cannot excuse in others. We turn our attention away from our own defects, and when we are forced by untoward events to consider them find it easy to condone them. For all I know we are right to do this; they are part of us and we must accept the good and the bad in ourselves together. But when we come to judge others it is not by ourselves as we really are that we judge them, but by an image that we have formed of ourselves from which we have left out everything that offends our vanity or would discredit us in the eyes of the world. To take a trivial instance: how scornful we are when we catch someone out telling a lie; but who can say that he has never told not one, but a hundred? We are shocked when we discover that great men were weak and petty, dishonest or selfish, sexually vicious, vain or intemperate; and many people think it disgraceful to disclose to the public its heroes' failings. There is not much to choose between men. They are all a hotchpotch of greatness and littleness, of virtue and vice, of nobility and baseness. Some have more strength of character, or more opportunity, and so in one direction or another give their instincts freer play, but potentially they are the same. For my part I do not think I am any better or any worse than most people, but I know that if I set down every action in my life and every thought that has crossed my mind the world would consider me a monster of depravity.

I wonder how anyone can have the face to condemn others when he reflects upon his own thoughts. A great part of our lives is occupied in reverie, and the more imaginative we are, the more varied and vivid this will be. How many of us could face having our reveries automatically registered and set before us? We should be overcome with shame. We should cry that we could not really be as mean, as wicked, as petty, as selfish, as obscene, as snobbish, as vain, as sentimental, as that. Yet surely our reveries are as much part of us as our actions, and if there were a being to whom our inmost thoughts were known we might just as well be held responsible for them as for our deeds. Men forget the horrible thoughts that wander through their own minds, and are indignant when they discover them in others. In Goethe's Wahrheit und Dichtung he relates how in his youth he could not bear the idea that his father was a middle-class lawyer in Frankfurt. He felt that noble blood must flow in his veins. So he sought to persuade himself that some prince travelling through the city had met and loved his mother, and that he was the offspring of the union. The editor of the copy I read wrote an indignant footnote on the subject. It seemed to him unworthy of so great a poet that he should impugn the undoubted virtue of his mother in order snobbishly to plume himself on his bastard aristocracy. Of course it was disgraceful, but it was not unnatural and I venture to say not uncommon. There must be few romantic, rebellious and imaginative boys who have not toyed with the idea that they could not be the son of their dull and respectable father, but ascribe the superiority they feel in themselves, according to their own idiosyncrasies, to an unknown poet, great statesman or ruling prince. The Olympian attitude of Goethe's later years inspires me with esteem; this confession arouses in me a warmer feeling. Because a man can write great works he is none the less a man.

It is, I suppose, these lewd, ugly, base and selfish thoughts, dwelling in their minds against their will, that have tormented the saints when their lives were devoted to good works and repentance had redeemed the sins of their past. St. Ignatius Loyola, as we know, when he went to Monserrat made a general confession and received absolution; but he continued to be obsessed by a sense of sin so that he was on the point of killing himself. Till his conversion he had led the ordinary life of the young man of good birth at that time; he was somewhat vain of his appearance, he had wenched and gambled; but at least on one occasion he had shown rare magnanimity and he had always been honourable, loyal, generous and brave. If peace was still denied him it looks as though it was his thoughts that he could not forgive himself. It would be a comfort to know that even the saints were thus afflicted. When I have seen the great ones of the earth, so upright and dignified, sitting in state I have often asked myself whether at such moments they ever remembered how their minds in solitude were sometimes occupied and whether it ever made them uneasy to think of the secrets that their subliminal self harboured. It seems to me that the knowledge that these reveries are common to all men should inspire one with tolerance to oneself as well as to others. It is well also if they enable us to look upon our fellows, even the most eminent and respectable, with humour and if they lead us to take ourselves not too seriously. When I have heard judges on the bench moralizing with unction I have asked myself whether it was possible for them to have forgotten their humanity so completely as their words suggested. I have wished that beside his bunch of flowers at the Old Bailey, his lordship had a packet of toilet paper. It would remind him that he was a man like any other.

17

I HAVE been called cynical. I have been accused of making men out worse than they are. I do not think I have done this. All I have done is to bring into prominence certain traits that many writers shut their eyes to. I think what has chiefly struck me in human beings is their lack of consistency. I have never seen people all of a piece. It has amazed me that the most incongruous traits should exist in the same person and for all that yield a plausible harmony. I have often asked myself how characteristics, seemingly irreconcilable, can exist in the same person. I have known crooks who were capable of self-sacrifice, sneak-thieves who were sweet-natured and harlots for whom it was a point of honour to give good value for money. The only explanation I can offer is that so instinctive is each one's conviction that he is unique in the world, and privileged, that he feels that, however wrong it might be for others, what he for his part does, of not natural and right, is at least venial. The contrast that I have found in people has interested me, but I do not think I have unduly emphasized it. The censure that has from time to time been passed on me is due perhaps to the fact that I have not expressly condemned what was bad in the characters of my invention and praised what was good. It must be a fault in me that I am not gravely shocked at the sins of others unless they personally affect me, and even when they do I have learnt at last generally to excuse them. It is meet not to expect too much of others. You should be grateful when they treat you well, but unperturbed when they treat you ill. 'For every one of us,' as the Athenian Stranger said, 'is made pretty much what he is by the bent of his desires and the nature of his soul.' It is want of imagination that prevents people from seeing things from any point of view but their own, and it is unreasonable to be angry with them because they lack this faculty.

I think I could be justly blamed if I saw only people's faults and were blind to their virtues. I am not conscious that this is the case. There is nothing more beautiful than goodness and it has pleased me very often to show how much of it there is in persons who by common standards would be relentlessly condemned. I have shown it because I have seen it. It has seemed to me sometimes to shine more brightly in them because it was surrounded by the darkness of sin. I take the goodness of the good for granted and I am amused when I discover their defects or their vices; I am touched when I see the goodness of the wicked and I am willing enough to shrug a tolerant shoulder at their wickedness. I am not my brother's keeper. I cannot bring myself to judge my fellows; I am content to observe them. My observation has led me to believe that, all in all, there is not so much difference between the good and the bad as the moralists would have us believe.

I have not on the whole taken people at their face value. I do not know if this coolness of scrutiny has been inherited from my fathers; they could hardly have been successful lawyers if they had not possessed a shrewdness that prevented them from being deceived by appearances;

or if I owe it to the lack in me of that joyful uprush of emotion on meeting people that makes many, as the saying is, take their geese for swans. It was certainly encouraged by my training as a medical student. I did not want to be a doctor. I did not want to be anything but a writer, but I was much too shy to say so, and in any case at that time it was unheard of that a boy of eighteen, belonging to a respectable family, should adopt literature as a profession. The notion was so preposterous that I never even dreamt of imparting it to anybody. I had always supposed that I should enter the law, but my three brothers, much older than I, were practising it and there did not seem room for me too.

18

I LEFT school early. I had been unhappy at the preparatory school to which I was sent on my father's death because it was at Canterbury and only six miles from Whitstable of which my uncle and guardian was vicar. It was an annex of the King's School, an ancient foundation, and to this when I was thirteen I duly went. After I had got out of the lower forms, the masters of which were frightening bullies, I was contented enough, and I was miserable when an illness forced me to spend a term in the South of France. My mother and her only sister had died of tuberculosis and when it was found that my lungs were affected my uncle and aunt were concerned. I was placed at a tutor's at Hyères. When I went back to Canterbury I did not like it so well. My friends had made new friends. I was lonely. I had been moved into a higher form in which, with three months lost, I could not find my place. My form-master nagged me. I persuaded my uncle that it would be very good for my lungs if instead of staying at school I spent the following winter on the Riviera and that it would be of value to me after that to go to Germany and learn German. I could continue to work there on the subjects which were necessary for me to get into Cambridge. He was a weak man and my arguments were specious. He did not much like me, for which I cannot blame him, since I do not think I was a likeable boy, and as it was my own money that was being spent on my education, he was willing enough to let me do as I chose. My aunt greatly favoured my plan. She was herself German, penniless but of noble birth; her family had a coat of arms with supporters and a great number of quarterings, of which she was primly arrogant. I have related elsewhere how, though but a poor clergyman's wife, she would not call on the wife of an opulent banker who had taken a house for the summer nearby because he was in trade. It was she who arranged that I should go to a family in Heidelberg whom she had heard of through her relations in Munich.

But when I came back from Germany, aged eighteen, I had very decided views of my own about my future. I had been happier than ever before. I had for the first time tasted freedom and I could not bear the thought of going to Cambridge and being subjected once more to restraint. I felt myself a man and I had a great eagerness to enter at once upon life. I felt that there was not a moment to waste. My uncle had always hoped that I would go into the church, though he should have known that, stammering as I did, no profession could have been more unsuitable; and when I told him that I wouldn't, he accepted with his usual indifference my refusal to go to Cambridge. I still remember the rather absurd arguments that were held about the calling I should adopt. A suggestion was made that I should become a civil servant and my uncle wrote to an old Oxford friend of his who held an important position in the Home Office for his advice. It was that, owing to the system of examinations and the class of persons it had introduced into the government service, it was now no place for a gentleman. That settled that. It was finally decided that I should become a doctor.

The medical profession did not interest me, but it gave me the chance of living in London and so gaining the experience of life that I hankered after. I entered St. Thomas's Hospital in the autumn of 1892. I found the first two years of the curriculum very dull and gave my work no more attention than was necessary to scrape through the examinations. I was an unsatisfactory student. But I had the freedom I yearned for. I liked having lodgings of my own, where I could be by myself; I took pride in making them pretty and comfortable. All my spare time, and much that I should have devoted to my medical studies, I spent reading and writing. I read enormously; I filled note-books with ideas for stories and plays, scraps of dialogue and reflections, very ingenuous ones, on what my reading and the various experiences that I was undergoing suggested to me. I entered little into the life of the hospital and made few friends there, for I was occupied with other things; but when, after two years, I became a clerk in the out-patient's departments I began to grow interested. In due course I started to work in the wards and then my interest so much increased that when I caught septic tonsillitis through doing a post-mortem on a corpse that was in an unreasonable state of decomposition and had to take to my bed, I could not wait to get well to resume my duties. I had to attend a certain number of confinements to get a certificate and this meant going into the slums of Lambeth, often into foul courts that the police hesitated to enter, but in which my black bag amply protected me: I found the work absorbing. For a short period I was on accident duty day and night to give first aid to urgent cases. It left me tired out but wonderfully exhilarated.

19

FOR HERE I was in contact with what I most wanted, life in the raw. In those three years I must have witnessed pretty well every emotion of which man is capable. It appealed to my dramatic instinct. It excited the novelist in me. Even now that forty years have passed I can remember certain people so exactly that I could draw a picture of them. Phrases that I heard then still linger on my ears. I saw how men died. I saw how they bore pain. I saw what hope looked like, fear and relief; I saw the dark lines that despair drew on a face; I saw courage and steadfastness. I saw faith shine in the eyes of those who trusted in what I could only think was an illusion and I saw the gallantry that made a man greet the prognosis of death with an ironic joke because he was too proud to let those about him see the terror of his soul.

At that time (a time to most people of sufficient ease, when peace seemed certain and prosperity secure) there was a school of writers who enlarged upon the moral value of suffering. They claimed that it was salutary. They claimed that it increased sympathy and enhanced the sensibilities. They claimed that it opened to the spirit new avenues of beauty and enabled it to get into touch with the mystical kingdom of God. They claimed that it strengthened the character, purified it from its human grossness and brought to him who did not avoid but sought it a more perfect happiness. Several books on these lines had a great success and their authors, who lived in comfortable homes, had three meals a day and were in robust health, gained much reputation. I set down in my note-books, not once or twice, but in a dozen places, the facts that I had seen. I knew that suffering did not ennoble; it degraded. It made men selfish, mean, petty and suspicious. It absorbed them in small things. It did not make them more than men; it made them less than men; and I wrote ferociously that we learn resignation not by our own suffering, but by the suffering of others.

All this was a valuable experience to me. I do not know a better training for a writer than to spend some years in the medical profession. I suppose that you can learn a good deal about human nature in a solicitor's office; but there on the whole you have to deal with men in full control of themselves. They lie perhaps as much as they lie to the doctor, but they lie more consistently, and it may be that for the solicitor it is not so necessary to know the truth. The interests he deals with, besides, are usually material. He sees human nature from a specialized standpoint. But the doctor, especially the hospital doctor, sees it bare. Reticences can generally be undermined;

43

very often there are none. Fear for the most part will shatter every defence; even vanity is unnerved by it. Most people have a furious itch to talk about themselves and are restrained only by the disinclination of others to listen. Reserve is an artificial quality that is developed in most of us but as the result of innumerable rebuffs. The doctor is discreet. It is his business to listen and no details are too intimate for his ears.

But of course human nature may be displayed before you and if you have not the eyes to see you will learn nothing. If you are hidebound with prejudice, if your temper is sentimental, you can go through the wards of a hospital and be as ignorant of man at the end as you were at the beginning. If you want to get any benefit from such an experience you must have an open mind and an interest in human beings. I look upon myself as very fortunate in that though I have never much liked men I have found them so interesting that I am almost incapable of being bored by them. I do not particularly want to talk and I am very willing to listen. I do not care if people are interested in me or not. I have no desire to impart any knowledge I have to others nor do I feel the need to correct them if they are wrong. You can get a great deal of entertainment out of tedious people if you keep your head. I remember being taken for a drive in a foreign country by a kind lady who wanted to show me round. Her conversation was composed entirely of truisms and she had so large a vocabulary of hackneyed phrases that I despaired of remembering them. But one remark she made has stuck in my memory as have few witticisms; we passed a row of little houses by the sea and she said to me: 'Those are week-end bungalows, if you understand what I mean; in other words they're bungalows that people go to on Saturdays and leave on Mondays.' I should have been sorry to miss that.

I do not want to spend too long a time with boring people, but then I do not want to spend too long a time with amusing ones. I find social intercourse fatiguing. Most persons, I think, are both exhilarated and rested by conversation; to me it has always been an effort. When

I was young and stammered, to talk for long singularly exhausted me, and even now that I have to some extent cured myself, it is a strain. It is a relief to me when I can get away and read a book.

20

I WOULD not claim for a moment that those years I spent at St. Thomas's Hospital gave me a complete knowledge of human nature. I do not suppose anyone can hope to have that. I have been studying it, consciously and subconsciously, for forty years and I still find men unaccountable; people I know intimately can surprise me by some action of which I never thought them capable or by the discovery of some trait exhibit a side of themselves that I never even suspected. It is possible that my training gave me a warped view, for at St. Thomas's the persons I came in contact with were for the most part sick and poor and ill-educated. I have tried to guard against this. I have tried also to guard against my own pre-possessions. I have no natural trust in others. I am more inclined to expect them to do ill than to do good. That is the price one has to pay for having a sense of humour. A sense of humour leads you to take pleasure in the discrepancies of human nature; it leads you to mistrust great professions and look for the unworthy motive that they conceal; the disparity between appearance and reality diverts you and you are apt when you cannot find it to create it. You tend to close your eyes to truth, beauty and goodness because they give no scope to your sense of the ridiculous. The humorist has a quick eye for the humbug; he does not always recognize the saint. But if to see men one-sidedly is a heavy price to pay for a sense of humour there is a compensation that has a value too. You are not angry with people when you laugh at them. Humour teaches tolerance, and the humorist, with a smile and perhaps a sigh, is more likely to shrug his shoulders than to condemn. He does not moralize, he is content to understand; and it is true that to understand is to pity and forgive.

But I must admit that, with these reservations that I have tried always to remember, the experience of all the years that have followed has only confirmed the observations on human nature that I made, not deliberately, for I was too young, but unconsciously, in the out-patients' departments and in the wards of St. Thomas's Hospital. I have seen men since as I saw them then, and thus have I drawn them. It may not be a true picture and I know that many have thought it an unpleasant one. It is doubtless partial, for naturally I have seen men through my own idiosyncrasies. A buoyant, optimistic, healthy and sentimental person would have seen the same people quite differently. I can only claim to have seen them coherently. Many writers seem to me not to observe at all, but to create their characters in stock sizes from images in their own fancy. They are like draughtsmen who draw their figures from recollections of the antique and have never attempted to draw from the living model. At their best they can only give living shape to the fantasies of their own minds. If their minds are noble they can give you noble figures and perhaps it does not matter if they lack the infinite complication of common life.

I have always worked from the living model. I remember that once in the Dissecting Room when I was going over my 'part' with the Demonstrator, he asked me what some nerve was and I did not know. He told me; whereupon I remonstrated, for it was in the wrong place. Nevertheless he insisted that it was the nerve I had been in vain looking for. I complained of the abnormality and he, smiling, said that in anatomy it was the normal that was uncommon. I was only annoyed at the time, but the remark sank into my mind and since then it has been forced upon me that it was true of man as well as of anatomy. The normal is what you find but rarely. The normal is an ideal. It is a picture that one fabricates of the average characteristics of men, and to find them all in a single man is hardly to be expected. It is this false picture that the writers I have spoken of take as their model and it is because they describe what is so exceptional that they seldom achieve the effect of life. Selfishness and kindliness, idealism and sensuality, vanity, shyness, disinterestedness, courage, laziness, nervousness, obstinacy, and diffidence, they can all exist in a single person and form a plausible harmony. It has taken a long time to persuade readers of the truth of this.

I do not suppose men in past centuries were any different from the men we know, but they must surely have appeared to their contemporaries more of a piece than they do to us now, or writers would not have thus represented them. It seemed reasonable to describe every man in his humour. The miser was nothing but miserly, the fop foppish, and the glutton gluttonous. It never occurred to anyone that the miser might be foppish and gluttonous; and yet we see constantly people who are; still less, that he might be an honest and upright man with a disinterested zeal for public service and a genuine passion for art. When novelists began to disclose the diversity that they had found in themselves or seen in others they were accused of maligning the human race. So far as I know the first novelist who did this with deliberate intention was Stendhal in Le Rouge et le Noir. Contemporary criticism was outraged. Even Sainte-Beuve, who needed only to look into his own heart to discover what contrary qualities could exist side by side in some kind of harmony, took him to task. Julien Sorel is one of the most interesting characters that a novelist has ever created. I do not think that Stendhal has succeeded in making him entirely plausible, but that, I believe, is due to causes that I shall mention in another part of this book. For the first three-quarters of the novel he is perfectly consistent. Sometimes he fills you with horror; sometimes he is entirely sympathetic; but he has an inner coherence, so that though you often shudder you accept.

But it was long before Stendhal's example bore fruit. Balzac, with all his genius, drew his characters after the old models. He gave them his own immense vitality so that you accept them as real; but in fact they are

47

humours as definitely as are the characters of old comedy. His people are unforgettable, but they are seen from the standpoint of the ruling passion that affected those with whom they were brought in contact. I suppose it is a natural prepossession of mankind to take people as though they were homogeneous. It is evidently less trouble to make up one's mind about a man one way or the other and dismiss suspense with the phrase, he's one of the best or he's a dirty dog. It is disconcerting to find that the saviour of his country may be stingy or that the poet who has opened new horizons to our consciousness may be a snob. Our natural egoism leads us to judge people in their relation to ourselves. We want them to be certain things to us, and for us that is what they are; because the rest of them is no good to us, we ignore it.

These reasons perhaps explain why there is so great a disinclination to accept the attempts to portray man with his incongruous and diverse qualities and why people turn away with dismay when candid biographers reveal the truth about famous persons. It is distressing to think that the composer of the quintet in the Meistersinger was dishonest in money matters and treacherous to those who had benefited him. But it may be that he could not have had great qualities if he had not also had great failings. I do not believe they are right who say that the defects of famous men should be ignored; I think it is better that we should know them. Then, though we are conscious of having faults as glaring as theirs, we can believe that that is no hindrance to our achieving also something of their virtues.

21

BESIDES TEACHING me something about human nature my training in a medical school furnished me with an elementary knowledge of science and scientific method. Till then I had been concerned only with art and litera-ture. It was a very limited knowledge, for the demands of the curriculum at that time were small, but at all events it showed me the road that led to a region of which I was completely ignorant. I grew familiar with certain principles. The scientific world of which I thus obtained a cursory glimpse was rigidly materialistic and because its conceptions coincided with my own prepossessions I embraced them with alacrity: 'For men,' as Pope observed, 'let them say what they will, never approve any other's sense, but as it squares with their own.' I was glad to learn that the mind of man (himself the product of natural causes) was a function of the brain subject like the rest of his body to the laws of cause and effect and that these laws were the same as those that governed the movements of star and atom. I exulted at the thought that the universe was no more than a vast machine in which every event was determined by a preceding event so that nothing could be other than it was. These conceptions not only appealed to my dramatic instinct; they filled me besides with a very delectable sense of liberation. With the ferocity of youth I welcomed the hypothesis of the Survival of the Fittest. It gave me much satisfaction to learn that the earth was a speck of mud whirling round a second-rate star which was gradually cooling; and that evolution, which had produced man, would by forcing him to adapt himself to his environment deprive him of all the qualities he had acquired but those that were necessary to enable him to combat the increasing cold till at last the planet, an icy cinder, would no longer support even a vestige of life. I believed that we were wretched puppets at the mercy of a ruthless fate; and that, bound by the inexorable laws of nature, we were doomed to take part in the ceaseless struggle for existence with nothing to look forward to but inevitable defeat. I learnt that men were moved by a savage egoism, that love was only the dirty trick nature played on us to achieve the continuation of the species, and I decided that, whatever aims men set themselves, they were deluded, for it was impossible for them to aim at anything but their own selfish pleasures. When once I happened to do a friend a good turn (for what reasons, since I knew that all our actions were purely selfish, I did not stop to think) and wanting to show his gratitude (which of course he had no business to feel, for my apparent kindness was rigidly determined) he asked me what I would like as a present, I answered without hesitation Herbert Spencer's First Principles. I read it with complacency. But I was impatient of Spencer's maudlin belief in progress: the world I knew was going from bad to worse and I was as pleased as Punch at the thought of my remote descendants, having long forgotten art and science and handicraft, cowering skin-clad in caverns as they watched the approach of the cold and eternal night. I was violently pessimistic. All the same, having abundant vitality, I was getting on the whole a lot of fun out of life. I was ambitious to make a name for myself as a writer. I exposed myself to every vicissitude that seemed to offer a chance of gaining the greater experience that I wanted and I read everything I could lay my hands on.

22

I LIVED at this time in a group of young men who had by nature gifts that seemed to me much superior to mine. They could write and draw and compose with a facility that aroused my envy. They had an appreciation of art and a critical instinct that I despaired of attaining. Of these some died without fulfilling the promise I thought they had and the rest have lived on without distinction. I know now that all they had was the natural creativity of youth. To write prose and verse, to hammer out little tunes on the piano and to draw and paint, are instinctive with a great many young persons. It is a form of play, due merely to the exuberance of their years, and is no more significant than a child's building of a castle on the sands. I suspect that it was my own ingenuousness that led me to admire so much the gifts of my friends. If I had been less ignorant I might have seen that the opinions that seemed to me so original were theirs only at second-hand and that their verses and their music owed more to a retentive memory than to a lively imagination. The point I want to make is that this facility is, if not universal, so common that one can draw no conclusions from it. Youth is the inspiration. One of the tragedies of the arts is the spectacle of the vast number of persons who have been misled by this passing fertility to devote their lives to the effort of creation. Their invention deserts them as they grow older, and they are faced with the long years before them in which, unfitted by now for a more humdrum calling, they harass their wearied brain to beat out material it is incapable of giving them. They are lucky when, with what bitterness we know, they can make a living in ways, like journalism or teaching, that are allied to the arts.

Of course it is from among those who possess by nature this facility that the artist is produced. Without it he cannot have talent; but it is only a part of talent. We start by living, each one of us, in the solitariness of our own minds and from the data given us and our communications with other minds we construct the outside world to suit our needs. Because we are all the result of one evolutionary process, and our environment is more or less the same, the constructions we make are roughly similar. For convenience and simplicity we accept them as identical and speak of a common world. The peculiarity of the artist is that he is in some particular different from other men and so the world of his construction is different too. It is this idiosyncrasy that is the better part of his equipment. When the picture he draws of his private world appeals to a certain number of persons, either by its strangeness, its intrinsic interest or its correspondence with their own prepossessions (for none of us is quite the same as his neighbour, only rather like, and not everyone accepts the world common to us all in every respect) his talent will be acknowledged. If he is a writer he will fulfil some need in the nature of his readers and they will lead with him a life of the spirit that satisfies them better than the life circumstances have forced on them. But there are others to whom this idiosyncrasy does not appeal. They have no patience with the world constructed by its instrumentality. It may actually revolt them. Then the artist has nothing to say to them and they will deny his talent.

I do not believe that genius is an entirely different thing from talent. I am not even sure that it depends on any great difference in the artist's natural gifts. For example, I do not think that Cervantes had an exceptional gift for writing; few people would deny him genius. Nor would it be easy in English literature to find a poet with a happier gift than Herrick and yet no one would claim that he had more than a delightful talent. It seems to me that what makes genius is the combination of natural gifts for creation with an idiosyncrasy that enables its possessor to see the world personally in the highest degree and yet with such catholicity that his appeal is not to this type of man or to that type, but to all men. His private world is that of common men, but ampler and more pithy. His communication is universal and though men may not be able to tell exactly what it signifies they feel that it is important. He is supremely normal. By a happy accident of nature seeing life with immense vivacity, as it were at concert pitch, he sees it, with its infinite diversity, in the healthy way that mankind at large sees it. In Matthew Arnold's phrase he sees it steadily and sees it whole. But genius arises once or twice in a century. The lesson of anatomy applies: there is nothing so rare as the normal. It is foolish to do as many do now and call a man a genius because he has written half a dozen clever plays or painted a score of good pictures. It is very well to have talent; few people have. With talent the artist will only reach the second class, but that need not disturb him for it contains the names of many whose works have uncommon merit. When you think it has produced such novels as Le Rouge et le Noir, such poems as The Shropshire Lad, such paintings as those of Watteau, there is not much to be ashamed of. Talent cannot reach the utmost heights, but it can show you many an unexpected and delicious view, an unfrequented dell, a bubbling brook or a romantic cavern, on the way that leads to them. The frowardness of human nature is such that it falters sometimes when it is bidden to take the broadest of all surveys of human nature. It will shrink from the splendour of Tolstoi's War and Peace to turn with complacency to Voltaire's Candide. It would be hard to live always with Michelangelo's ceiling in the Sistine Chapel, but anyone could do with one of Constable's pictures of Salisbury Cathedral.

My sympathies are limited. I can only be myself, and partly by nature, party by the circumstances of my life, it is a partial self. I am not a social person. I cannot get drunk and feel a great love for my fellow-men. Convivial amusement has always somewhat bored me. When people sitting in an ale-house or drifting down the river in a boat start singing I am silent. I have never even sung a hymn. I do not much like being touched and I have always to make a slight effort over myself not to draw away when someone links his arm in mine. I can never forget myself. The hysteria of the world repels me and I never feel more aloof than when I am in the midst of a throng surrendered to a violent feeling of mirth or sorrow. Though I have been in love a good many times I have never experienced the bliss of requited love. I know that this is the best thing that life can offer and it is a thing that almost all men, though perhaps only for a short time, have enjoyed. I have most loved people who cared little or nothing for me and when people have loved me I have been embarrassed. It has been a predicament that I have not quite known how to deal with. In order not to hurt their feelings I have often acted a passion that I did not feel. I have tried, with gentleness when possible, and if not, with irritation, to escape from the trammels with which their love bound me. I have been jealous of my independence. I am incapable of complete surrender. And so, never having felt some of the fundamental emotions of normal men, it is impossible that my work should have the intimacy, the broad human touch and the animal serenity which the greatest writers alone can give.

23

IT IS dangerous to let the public behind the scenes. They are easily disillusioned and then they are angry with you, for it was the illusion they loved; they do not understand that what interests you is the way in which you have created the illusion. Anthony Trollope ceased to be read for thirty years because he confessed that he wrote at regular hours and took care to get the best price he could for his work.

But for me the race now is nearly run and it would ill become me to conceal the truth. I do not want anyone to think better of me than I deserve. Let those who like me take me as I am and let the rest leave me. I have more character than brains and more brains than specific gifts. I said something of this sort many years ago to a charming and distinguished critic. I do not know what led me to do so, since I am not much inclined to talk about myself in general company. It was at Montdidier, during the first months of the war, and we were lunching there on our way to Péronne. We had been very hard-worked for some days and it was a pleasure to linger over a meal that seemed to our healthy appetites uncommonly good. I suppose I was flushed with wine and I daresay excited by the discovery, from a statue in the market-place, that Montdidier was the birthplace of Parmentier, who introduced the potato into France. Anyhow as we idled over our coffee and liqueurs I was moved to give an acute and candid analysis of my talent. I was disconcerted some years later to read it, almost in my very words, in the columns of an important paper. I was a trifle vexed, for it is a very different thing to tell the truth about yourself and to have somebody else tell it, and I should have liked the critic to do me the compliment of saying that he had heard it all from my own lips. But I chid myself. I thought it very natural that he should like to think that he had so much perspicacity. And it was the truth. It has been a little unfortunate for me, since the critic is deservedly influential and what he said in this article has been very generally repeated. In another moment of frankness I informed my readers that I was unusually competent. One would think that except for this the critics would never have discovered it; but since then the adjective has been much and depreciatingly applied to me. It has seemed strange to me that so many people concerned, though only at second-hand, with the arts should regard competence with so little favour.

I am told that there are natural singers and made singers. Though of course he must have something of a voice the made singer owes the better part of his accomplishment to training; with taste and musical ability he can eke out the relative poverty of his organ and his singing can afford a great deal of pleasure, especially to the connoisseur; but he will never move you as you are moved to ecstasy by the pure, bird-like notes of the natural singer. The natural singer may be inadequately trained, he may have neither tact nor knowledge, he may outrage all the canons of art, but such is the magic of his voice that you are captivated. You forgive the liberties he takes, his vulgarities, his appeals to obvious emotion, when those heavenly sounds enchant your ear. I am a made writer. But it would be vanity if I thought that such results as I have achieved on myself were due to a design that I deliberately carried out. I was drawn to various courses by very simple motives and it is only on looking back that I discover myself subconsciously working to a certain end. The end was to develop my character and so make up for the deficiencies in my natural gifts.

I have a clear and logical brain, but not a very subtle nor a very powerful one. For long I wished it were better. I used to get exasperated because it would not do for me nearly as much as I wished. I was like a mathematician who could do no more than add and subtract and though he wanted to tackle all manner of complicated operations knew that he simply had not the capacity. It took me a long time to resign myself to making the best of what I had. I think it was a good enough brain to have brought me success in whatever profession I had adopted. I am not one of those persons who is a fool at everything but his own speciality. In law, medicine and politics a clear mind and insight into men are useful.

I have had one advantage; I have never wanted a subject. I have always had more stories in my head than I ever had time to write. I have often heard writers complain that they wanted to write but had nothing to write about, and I remember one distinguished author telling me that she was reading through some book in which were epitomized all the plots that had ever been used in order to find a theme. I have never found myself in such a predicament. Swift, as we know, who claimed that he could write on any subject whatever, when he was challenged to write a discourse on a broomstick acquitted himself very creditably. I am almost inclined to say that I could not spend an hour in anyone's company without getting the material to write at least a readable story about him. It is pleasant to have so many stories in mind that whatever your mood you have one upon which, for an hour or two, for a week or so, you can let your fancy linger. Reverie is the groundwork of creative imagination; it is the privilege of the artist that with him it is not as with other men an escape from reality, but the means by which he accedes to it. His reverie is purposeful. It affords him a delight in comparison with which the pleasures of sense are pale and it affords him the assurance of his freedom. One cannot wonder if sometimes he is unwilling to exchange its enjoyment for the drudgery and loss of execution.

But though I have had variety of invention, and this is not strange since it is the outcome of the variety of mankind, I have had small power of imagination. I have taken living people and put them into the situations, tragic or comic, that their characters suggested. I might well say that they invented their own stories. I have been incapable of those great, sustained flights that carry the author on broad pinions into a celestial sphere. My fancy, never very strong, has been hampered by my sense of probability. I have painted easel pictures, not frescoes.

24

I HEARTILY wish that in my youth I had had someone of good sense to direct my reading. I sigh when I reflect on the amount of time I have wasted on books that were of no great profit to me. What little guidance I had I owe to a young man who came to live with the same family in Heidelberg as I was living with. I will call him Brown. He was then twenty-six. After leaving Cambridge he was called to the bar, but he had a little money, enough to live on in those inexpensive days, and finding the law distasteful he had made up his mind to devote himself to literature. He came to Heidelberg to learn German. I knew him till his death forty years later. For twenty years he amused himself with thinking what he would write when he really got down to it and for another twenty with what he could have written if the fates had been kinder. He wrote a good deal of verse. He had neither imagination, nor passion; and he had a defective ear. He spent some years translating those dialogues of Plato that had been already most often translated. I doubt, however, if he ever got to the end of one. He was completely devoid of will-power. He was sentimental and vain. Though short he was handsome, with finely cut features and curly hair; he had pale blue eyes and a wistful expression. He looked as one imagines a poet should look. As an old man, after a life of complete indolence, bald and emaciated, he had an ascetic air so that you might have taken him for a don who had spent long years in ardent and disinterested research. The spirituality of his expression suggested the tired scepticism of a philosopher who had plumbed the secrets of existence and discovered nothing but vanity. Having gradually wasted his small fortune, he preferred to live on the generosity of others rather than work, and often he found it difficult to make both ends meet. His self-complacency never deserted him. It enabled him to endure poverty with resignation and failure with indifference. I do not think he ever had an inkling that he was an outrageous sham. His whole life was a lie, but when he was dying, if he had known he was going to, which mercifully he didn't, I am convinced he would have looked upon it as well-spent. He had charm, he was devoid of envy, and though too selfish to do anyone a good turn, he was incapable of unkindness. He had a real appreciation of literature. During the long walks we took together over the hills of Heidelberg he talked to me of books. He talked to me of Italy and Greece, neither of which in point of fact he knew, but he fired my young imagination and I began to learn Italian. I accepted everything he told me with the fervour of the proselyte. I should not blame him because he inspired me with a passionate admiration for certain works that time has shown to be not so admirable. When he arrived he found me reading Tom Jones, which I had got out of the public library, and he told me that of course there was no harm in it, but I should do better to read Diana of the Crossways. Even then he was a Platonist and he gave me Shelley's translation of the Symposium. He talked to me of Renan, Cardinal Newman and Matthew Arnold. But Matthew Arnold, he thought, was a bit of a philistine himself. He talked to me of Swinburne's Poems and Ballads and of Omar Khayyám. He knew a great many of the quatrains by heart and recited them to me on our walks. I was divided between enthusiasm for the romantic epicureanism of the matter and the embarrassment occasioned by Brown's delivery, for he recited poetry like a high-church curate intoning the Litany in an ill-lit crypt. But the two writers that it was really necessary to admire if you would be a person of culture and not a British philistine were Walter Pater and George Meredith. I was very ready to do what I was told to achieve this desirable end and incredible as it must seem I read The Shaving of Shagpat with roars of laughter. It seemed to me superlatively funny. Then I read the novels of George Meredith one after the other. I thought them wonderful; but not so wonderful as even to myself I pretended. My admiration was fictitious. I admired because it was the part of a cultured young man to admire.

I intoxicated myself with my own enthusiasm. I would not listen to the still small voice within me that carped. Now I know that there is a great deal of fustian in these novels. But the strange thing is that, reading them again, I recapture the days when I first read them. They are rich for me now with sunny mornings and my awakening intelligence and the delicious dreams of youth, so that even as I close a novel of Meredith's, Evan Harrington for instance, and decide that its insincerity is exasperating, its snobbishness loathsome, its verbosity intolerable and I will never read another, my heart melts and I think it's grand.

On the other hand I have no such feeling about Walter Pater whom I read at the same time and with a similar excitement. No pleasant associations give him for me a merit to which he has no claim. I find him as dull as a picture of Alma Tadema. It is strange that one can ever have admired that prose. It does not flow. There is no air in it. A careful mosaic constructed by someone without great technical skill to decorate the walls of a station dining-room. Pater's attitude towards the life about him, cloistered, faintly supercilious, gentlemanly, donnish in short, repels me. Art should be appreciated with passion and violence, not with a tepid, deprecating elegance that fears the censoriousness of a common-room. But Walter Pater was a feeble creature: it is unnecessary to condemn him with intensity. I dislike him not for himself, but because he is an example of a type in the literary world that is common and detestable. This is the person who is filled with the conceit of culture.

The value of culture is its effect on character. It avails nothing unless it ennobles and strengthens that. Its use is for life. Its aim is not beauty but goodness. Too often, as we know, it gives rise to self-complacency. Who has not seen the scholar's thin-lipped smile when he corrects a misquotation and the connoisseur's pained look when someone praises a picture he does not care for? There is no more merit in having read a thousand books than in having ploughed a thousand fields. There is no more merit in being able to attach a correct description to a picture than in being able to find out what is wrong with a stalled motor-car. In each case it is special knowledge. The stockbroker has his knowledge too and so has the artizan. It is a silly prejudice of the intellectual that his is the only one that counts. The True, the Good and the Beautiful are not the perquisites of those who have been to expensive schools, burrowed in libraries and frequented museums. The artist has no excuse when he uses others with condescension. He is a fool if he thinks his knowledge is more important than theirs and an oaf if he cannot comfortably meet them on an equal footing. Matthew Arnold did a great disservice to culture when he insisted on its opposition to philistinism.

25

AT EIGHTEEN I knew French, German and some Italian, but I was extremely uneducated and I was deeply conscious of my ignorance. I read everything that came my way. My curiosity was such that I was as willing to read a history of Peru or the reminiscences of a cowboy as a treatise on Provençal poetry or the Confessions of St. Augustine. I suppose it gained me a certain amount of general knowledge which is useful for the novelist to have. One never knows when an out of the way bit of information will come in handy. I made lists of what I read and one of these lists by some accident I still have. It is my reading for two months and, but that I made it only for myself, I could not believe that it was veracious. It shows that I read three of Shakespeare's plays, two volumes of Mommsen's History of Rome, a large part of Lanson's Littérature Française, two or three novels, some of the French classics, a couple of scientific works and a play of Ibsen's. I was indeed the industrious apprentice. During the time I was at St. Thomas's Hospital I went systematically through English, French, Italian and Latin literature. I read a lot of history, a little philosophy and a good deal of science. My curiosity was too great to allow me to give much time to reflect upon what I read; I could hardly wait to finish one book, so eager was

I to begin another. This was always an adventure, and I would start upon a famous work as excitedly as a reasonable young man would go in to bat for his side or a nice girl go to a dance. Now and then journalists in search of copy ask me what is the most thrilling moment of my life. If I were not ashamed to, I might answer that it is the moment when I began to read Goethe's Faust. I have never quite lost this feeling, and even now the first pages of a book sometimes send the blood racing through my veins. To me reading is a rest as to other people conversation or a game of cards. It is more than that; it is a necessity, and if I am deprived of it for a little while I find myself as irritable as the addict deprived of his drug. I would sooner read a time-table or a catalogue than nothing at all. That is putting it too low. I have spent many delightful hours poring over the price-list of the Army and Navy Stores, the lists of second-hand booksellers and the A B C. All these are redolent of romance. They are much more entertaining than half the novels that are written.

I have put books aside only because I was conscious that time was passing and that it was my business to live. I have gone into the world because I thought it was necessary in order to get the experience without which I could not write, but I have gone into it also because I wanted experience for its own sake. It did not seem to me enough only to be a writer. The pattern I had designed for myself insisted that I should take the utmost part I could in this fantastic affair of being a man. I desired to feel the common pains and enjoy the common pleasures that are part of the common human lot. I saw no reason to subordinate the claims of sense to the tempting lure of spirit and I was determined to get whatever fulfilment I could out of social intercourse and human relations, out of food, drink and fornication, luxury, sport, art, travel, and as Henry James says, whatever. But it was an effort and I have always returned to my books and my own company with relief.

And yet, though I have read so much, I am a bad reader. I read slowly and I am a poor skipper. I find it difficult to leave a book, however bad and however much it bores me, unfinished. I could count on my fingers the number of books that I have not read from cover to cover. On the other hand there are few books that I have read twice. I know very well that there are many of which I cannot get the full value on a single reading, but in that they have given me all I was capable of getting at the time, and this, though I may forget their details, remains a permanent enrichment. I know people who read the same book over and over again. It can only be that they read with their eyes and not with their sensibility. It is a mechanical exercise like the Tibetan's turning of a praying-wheel. It is doubtless a harmless occupation, but they are wrong if they think it an intelligent one.

26

IN MY youth, when my instinctive feeling about a book differed from that of authoritative critics I did not hesitate to conclude that I was wrong. I did not know how often critics accept the conventional view and it never occurred to me that they could talk with assurance of what they did not know very much about. It was long before I realized that the only thing that mattered to me in a work of art was what I thought about it. I have acquired now a certain confidence in my own judgement, for I have noticed that what I felt instinctively forty years ago about the writers I read then, and what I would not heed because it did not agree with current opinion, is now pretty generally accepted. For all that I still read a great deal of criticism, for I think it a very agreeable form of literary composition. One does not always want to be reading to the profit of one's soul and there is no pleasanter way of idling away an hour or two than reading a volume of criticism. It is diverting to agree; it is diverting to differ; and it is always interesting to know what an intelligent man has to say about some writer, Henry More, for instance, or Richardson, whom you have never had occasion to read.

But the only important thing in a book is the meaning it has for you; it may have other and much more profound meanings for the critic, but at second-hand they can be of small service to you. I do not read a book for the book's sake, but for my own. It is not my business to judge it, but to absorb what I can of it, as the amœba absorbs a particle of a foreign body, and what I cannot assimilate has nothing to do with me. I am not a scholar, a student or a critic; I am a professional writer and now I read only what is useful to me professionally. Anyone can write a book that will revolutionize the ideas that have been held for centuries on the Ptolemys and I shall contentedly leave it unread; he can describe an incredibly adventurous journey in the heart of Patagonia and I shall remain ignorant of it. There is no need for the writer of fiction to be an expert on any subject but his own; on the contrary, it is hurtful to him, since, human nature being weak, he is hard put to it to resist the temptation of inappositely using his special knowledge. The novelist is ill-advised to be too technical. The practice, which came into fashion in the nineties, of using a multitude of cant terms is tiresome. It should be possible to give verisimilitude without that, and atmosphere is dearly bought at the price of tediousness. The novelist should know something about the great issues that occupy men, who are his topics, but it is generally enough if he knows a little. He must avoid pedantry at all costs. But even at that the field is vast and I have tried to limit myself to such works as were significant to my purpose. You can never know enough about your characters. Biographies and reminiscences, technical works, will give you often an intimate detail, a telling touch, a revealing hint, that you might never have got from a living model. People are hard to know. It is a slow business to induce them to tell you the particular thing about themselves that can be of use to you. They have the disadvantage that often you cannot look at them and put them aside, as you can a book, and you have to read the whole volume, as it were, only to learn that it had nothing much to tell you.

27

YOUNG PERSONS, who are anxious to write, sometimes pay me the compliment of asking me to tell them of certain books necessary for them to read. I do. They seldom read them, for they seem to have little curiosity. They do not care what their predecessors have done. They think they know everything that it is necessary to know of the art of fiction when they have read two or three novels by Mrs. Woolf, one by E. M. Forster, several by D. H. Lawrence and, oddly enough, the Forsyte Saga. It is true that contemporary literature has a vividness of appeal that classical literature can never have and it is well for a young writer to know what his contemporaries are writing about and how. But there are fashions in literature and it is not easy to tell what intrinsic value there is in a style of writing that happens to be the vogue at the moment. An acquaintance with the great works of the past serves as a very good standard of comparison. I have sometimes wondered whether it is due to their ignorance that many young writers, notwithstanding their facility and cleverness, their skilful technique, so frequently fizzle out. They write two or three books that are not only brilliant, but mature, and then they are done for. But that is not what enriches the literature of a country. For that you must have writers who can produce not just two or three books, but a great body of work. Of course it will be uneven, because so many fortunate circumstances must go together to produce a masterpiece; but a masterpiece is more likely to come as the culminating point of a laborious career than as the lucky fluke of untaught genius. The writer can only be fertile if he renews himself and he can only renew himself if his soul is constantly enriched by fresh experience. There is no more fruitful source of this than the enchanting exploration of the great literatures of the past.

For the production of a work of art is not the result of a miracle. It requires preparation. The soil, be it ever so rich, must be fed. By taking thought, by deliberate effort, the artist must enlarge, deepen and diversify his personality. Then the soil must lie fallow. Like the bride of Christ, the artist waits for the illumination that shall bring forth a new spiritual life. He goes about his ordinary avocations with patience; the subconscious does its mysterious business; and then, suddenly springing, you might think from nowhere, the idea is produced. But like the corn that was sown on stony ground it may easily wither away; it must be tended with anxious care. All the power of the artist's mind must be set to work on it, all his technical skill, all his experience, and whatever he has in him of character and individuality, so that with infinite pains he may present it with the completeness that is fitting to it.

But I am not impatient with the young when, only at their request, I insist, I advise them to read Shakespeare and Swift, and they tell me that they read Gulliver's Travels in their nursery and Henry IV at school; and if they find Vanity Fair unendurable and Anna Karenina footling it is their own affair. No reading is worth while unless you enjoy it. There is at least this to be said for them that they do not suffer from the self-conceit of knowledge. They are not withdrawn by a wide culture from sympathy with the common run of men who are after all their material. They are nearer to their fellows and the art they practise is not a mystery, but a craft on the same footing as any other. They write novels and plays as unaffectedly as other men build motor-cars. This is much to the good. For the artist, the writer especially, in the solitariness of his own mind constructs a world that is different from other men's; the idiosyncrasy that makes him a writer separates him from them and the paradox emerges that though his aim is to describe them truthfully his gift prevents him from knowing them as they really are. It is as though he wanted urgently to see a certain thing and by the act of looking at it drew before it a veil that obscured it. The writer stands outside the very action he is engaged in. He is the comedian who never quite loses himself in the part, for he is at the same time spectator and actor. It is all very well to say that poetry is emotion remembered in tranquillity; but a poet's emotion is specific, a poet's rather than a man's, and it is never quite disinterested. That is why women with their instinctive common sense have so often found the love of poets unsatisfying. It may be that the writers of the present day, who seem to be so much nearer to their raw material, ordinary men among ordinary men, rather than artists in an alien crowd, may break down the barrier that their peculiar gift cannot but raise and so come nearer to the plain truth than has ever been done before.

28

I HAD my full share of the intellectual's arrogance and if, as I hope, I have lost it, I must ascribe it not to my own virtue or wisdom but to the chance that made me more of a traveller than most writers. I am attached to England, but I have never felt myself very much at home there. I have always been shy with English people. To me England has been a country where I had obligations that I did not want to fulfil and responsibilities that irked me. I have never felt entirely myself till I had put at least the Channel between my native country and me. Some fortunate persons find freedom in their own minds; I, with less spiritual power than they, find it in travel. While still at Heidelberg I managed to visit a good many places in Germany (at Munich I saw Ibsen drinking a glass of beer at the Maximilianerhof and with a scowl on his face reading the paper) and I went to Switzerland; but the first real journey I made was to Italy. I went primed with much reading of Walter Pater, Ruskin and John Addington Symonds. I had the six weeks of the Easter vacation at my disposal and twenty pounds in my pocket. After going to Genoa and Pisa, where I trudged the interminable distance to sit for a while on the pine wood in which Shelley read Sophocles and wrote verses on a guitar, I settled down for the inside of a month in Florence in the house of a widow lady, with whose daughter I read the Purgatorio, and spent laborious days, Ruskin in hand, visiting the sights. I admired everything that Ruskin told me to admire (even that horrible tower of Giotto) and turned away in disgust from what he condemned. Never can he have had a more ardent disciple. After that I went to Venice, Verona and Milan. I returned to England very much pleased with myself and actively contemptuous of anyone who did not share my views (and Ruskin's) of Botticelli and Bellini. I was twenty.

A year later I went to Italy again, travelling as far down as Naples, and discovered Capri. It was the most enchanting spot I had ever seen and the following summer I spent the whole of my vacation there. Capri was then little known. There was no funicular from the beach to the town. Few people went there in summer and you could get board and lodging, with wine included, and from your bedroom window a view of Vesuvius, for four shillings a day. There was a poet there then, a Belgian composer, my friend from Heidelberg, Brown, a painter or two, a sculptor (Harvard Thomas) and an American colonel who had fought on the southern side in the Civil War. I listened with transport to conversations, up at Anacapri at the colonel's house, or at Morgano's, the wine shop just off the Piazza, when they talked of art and beauty, literature and Roman history. I saw two men fly at one another's throats because they disagreed over the poetic merit of Heredia's sonnets. I thought it all grand. Art, art for art's sake, was the only thing that mattered in the world; and the artist alone gave this ridiculous world significance. Politics, commerce, the learned professions—what did they amount to from the standpoint of the Absolute? They might disagree, these friends of mine (dead, dead every jack one of them), about the value of a sonnet or the excellence of a Greek bas-relief (Greek, my eye! I tell you it's a Roman copy and if I tell you a thing it is so); but they were all agreed about this, that they burned with a hard, gem-like flame. I was too shy to tell them that I had written a novel and was half-way through another and it was a great mortification to me, burning as I was too with a hard, gem-like flame, to be treated as a philistine who cared for nothing but dissecting dead bodies and would seize an unguarded moment to give his best friend an enema.

29

PRESENTLY I was qualified. I had already published a novel and it had had an unexpected success. I thought my fortune was made, and, abandoning medicine to become a writer, I went to Spain. I was then twenty-three. I was much more ignorant than are, it seems to me, young men of that age at the present day. I settled down in Seville. I grew a moustache, smoked Filipino cigars, learnt the guitar, bought a broad-brimmed hat with a flat crown, in which I swaggered down the Sierpes, and hankered for a flowing cape, lined with green and red velvet. But on account of the expense I did not buy it. I rode about the countryside on a horse lent me by a friend. Life was too pleasant to allow me to give an undivided attention to literature. My plan was to spend a year there till I had learnt Spanish, then go to Rome which I knew only as a tripper and perfect my superficial knowledge of Italian, follow that up with a journey to Greece where I intended to learn the vernacular as an approach to ancient Greek, and finally go to Cairo and learn Arabic. It was an ambitious programme, but I am glad now that I did not carry it out. I duly went to Rome (where I wrote my first play) but then I went back to Spain; for something had occurred that I had not anticipated. I fell in love with Seville and the life one led there and incidentally with a young thing with green eyes and a gay smile (but I got over that) and I could not resist its lure. I returned year after year. I wandered through the white and silent streets and strolled along the Guadalquivir, I dawdled about the Cathedral, I went to bull-fights and made light love to pretty little creatures whose demands on me were no more than my exiguous means could satisfy. It was heavenly to live in Seville in the flower of one's youth. I postponed my education to a more convenient moment. The result is that I have never read the Odyssey but in English and I have never achieved my ambition to read A Thousand Nights and a Night in Arabic.

When the intelligentsia took up Russia I, remembering that Cato had begun to learn Greek when he was eighty, set about learning Russian, but I had by then lost my youthful enthusiasm; I never got farther than being able to read the plays of Chekov and have long since forgotten the little I knew. I think now that these schemes of mine were a trifle nonsensical. Words are not important, but their meanings, and it is of no spiritual advantage that I can see to know half a dozen languages. I have met polyglots; I have not noticed that they were wiser than the rest of us. It is convenient if you are travelling in a country to have a sufficient smattering of its speech to find your way about and get what you want to eat; and if it has a considerable literature it is pleasant to be able to read it. But such a knowledge as this can be acquired easily. To attempt to learn more is futile. Unless you devote your whole life to it, you will never learn to speak the language of another country to perfection; you will never know its people and its literature with complete intimacy. For they, and the literature which is their expression, are wrought, not only of the actions they perform and the words they use, neither of which offer great difficulty, but of ancestral instincts, shades of feeling that they have absorbed with their mothers' milk, and innate attitudes which the foreigner can never quite seize. It is hard enough for us to know our own people; we deceive ourselves, we English especially, if we think we can know those of other lands. For the sea-girt isle sets us apart and the link that a common religion gave, which once mitigated our insularity, was snapped with the Reformation. It seems hardly worth while to take much trouble to acquire a knowledge that can never be more than superficial. I think then it is merely waste of time to learn more than a smattering of foreign tongues. The only exception I would make to this is French. For French is the common language of educated men and it is certainly convenient to speak it well enough to be able to treat of any subject of discourse that may arise. It has a great literature; other countries, with the exception of England, have great writers, rather than a great literature; and its influence on the rest of the world has, till the last twenty years, been profound. It is very well to be able to read French as easily as if it were your native tongue. There are limits, however, to the excellence with which you should allow yourself to speak it. As a matter of practice it is good to be on your guard against an Englishman who speaks French perfectly; he is very likely to be a card-sharper or an attaché in the diplomatic service.

30

I WAS never stage-struck. I have known dramatists who wandered in every night to the theatre in which their play was being acted. They said they did it in order to see that the cast was not getting slack: I suspect it was because they could never hear their own words spoken often enough. Their delight was to sit in a dressing-room during the intervals and talk over this scene or the other, wondering why it had fallen flat that night or congratulating themselves on how well it had gone, and watch an actor make up. They never ceased to find the theatrical gossip of the day absorbing. They loved the theatre and everything connected with it. They had grease-paint in their bones.

I have never been like that. I like a theatre best when it is under dust-sheets, the auditorium in darkness, and the unset stage, with the flats stacked against the back wall, is lit only by footlights. I have passed many happy hours at rehearsals; I have liked their easy camaraderie, the hurried lunch at a restaurant round the corner with a member of the cast and the cup of strong bitter tea, with thick bread and butter, brought in by the charwoman at four o'clock. I have never quite lost that little thrill of surprised amusement I felt when in my first play I heard grown men and women repeat the lines that had come so easily to my pen. It has interested me to watch the way in which a part grows in the actor's hands from the first lifeless reading of the typescript to something like the character that I have seen in my mind's eye. I have been diverted by the important discussions about the exact place where a piece of furniture should stand, the self-sufficiency of the director, the tantrums of an actress displeased with her positions, the artfulness of old players determined to get the centre of the stage for their scene, and the desultory talk about any subject that came to hand. But the consummation is the dress-rehearsal. There are half a dozen people in the front-row of the dress-circle. They are the dressmakers, subdued as though they were in church, but very business-like; they exchange short, sharp whispers with one another during the performance and make little significant gestures. You know that they are speaking of the length of a skirt, the cut of a sleeve or the feather in a hat; and the moment the curtain falls, the pins already in their mouths, they hurry through the door on to the stage. The director* shouts 'curtain up' and when it rises an actress snatches herself away from an agitated colloquy with two grim ladies in black.

"Oh, Mr. Thing," she calls out, "I know that passementerie is wrong, but Madame Floss says she'll take it off and put a bit of lace instead."

In the stalls are the photographers, the management and the man from the box-office, the mothers of the actresses in the cast and the wives of the actors, your own agent, a girl-friend of yours, and three or four old actors who haven't had a part for twenty years. It is the perfect audience. After each act the director reads out the remarks he has jotted down. There is a row with the electrician who, with nothing to do but attend to his switches, has turned on the wrong ones; and the author is indignant with him for being so careless and at the same time indulgent because he has a notion that the electrician only forgot his work because he was so

* I use the American word director rather than the English one, producer, because I think it better describes what should be the function of the person in question.

absorbed in the play. Perhaps a little scene is repeated; then effective positions are arranged and with sudden blares of flash-light photographs are taken. The curtain is lowered to set the scene for the next act and the cast separate to their dressing-rooms to change. The dressmakers vanish and the old actors slink round the corner to have a drink. The management despondently smoke gaspers, the wives and mothers of the cast talk to one another in undertones and the author's agent reads the racing news in the evening paper. It is all unreal and exciting. At last the dressmakers filter through the fire-proof door and resume their seats, the representatives of rival firms at a haughty distance from one another, and the stage-manager puts his head round the curtain.

"All ready, Mr. Thing," he says.

"All right. Fire away. Curtain up."

But the dress-rehearsal was the last pleasure my play ever had to give me. At the first nights of my early plays I was on tenterhooks, for on their result my future depended. When Lady Frederick was produced I had reached the end of the little money I had come into when I was twenty-one, my novels did not bring me in enough to live upon, and I could earn nothing by journalism. I had been given a little reviewing now and then and once persuaded an editor to let me do the notice of a play, but I evidently had no gifts in that direction; indeed, the editor in question told me that I had no sense of the theatre. If Lady Frederick was a failure it seemed to me that there was nothing for me but to go back to the hospital for a year to refresh my knowledge of medicine and then get a post as surgeon on a ship. At that time this was a position not much sought after and few men with London degrees applied for it. Later, when I had become a successful dramatist, I went to first nights with my senses alert to discern from the reactions of the public whether there was any falling off in my ability. I did my best to lose myself in the audience. For the audience a first night is a more or less interesting event which they take between a snack at seven-thirty and supper at eleven, and the success or failure of which is no great matter. I tried to go to my own first nights as though they were somebody else's; but even at that I found it a disagreeable experience. It did me no good to hear the laughter that rewarded a happy jest or the applause that broke out on the fall of the curtain when an act had pleased. The fact is that, even in my lightest pieces, I had put in so much of myself that I was embarrassed to hear it disclosed to a crowd of people. Because they were words I had written myself they had for me an intimacy that I shrank from sharing with all and sundry. This unreasonable feeling I have had even when I have gone to see a play of mine in a translation and have sat in the theatre as an entirely unknown member of the public. Indeed I should never have gone to see my plays at all, on the first night or any other, if I had not thought it necessary to see the effect they had on the audience in order to learn how to write them.

31

THE ACTOR'S calling is a hard one. I am not speaking now of the young women who go on the stage because they have a pretty face and if good looks were a qualification for typists might just as well have gone into an office, or of the young men who do so because they have a good figure and no particular aptitude for anything else. They drift in and out of the profession; the women marry and the men get into a wine-merchant's office or take up interior decoration. I am speaking of the actors by vocation. They have a natural gift and the desire to use it. It is a profession that requires assiduous labour to achieve proficiency, so that by the time an actor knows how to act any sort of part he is often too old to act any but a few; it requires boundless patience; it is fraught with disappointments. Long stretches of enforced idleness must be endured. The prizes are few and can be held but for a brief period. The rewards are inadequate. The actor is at the mercy of fortune and the inconstant favour of the public. He is forgotten as soon as he ceases to please. Then it will avail him nothing to have been the idol of the crowd. He can starve for all they care. It is when I think of this that I find it easy to be indulgent to the actor's airs and graces, his exigence and vanity, when he is on the crest of the wave. Let him be flamboyant and absurd if he likes. It all lasts such a little while. And after all his egotism is part of his talent.

There was a period when the stage was the doorway to romance and everyone connected with it seemed exciting and mysterious. In the civilized world of the eighteenth century the actors gave life a touch of fantasy. Their disorderly existence was a lure to the imagination in the Age of Reason and the heroic parts they played, the verse they spoke, invested them with a halo. In Goethe's Wilhelm Meister, that wonderful and neglected book, you can see with what tenderness the poet regarded what can have been nothing but a second-rate touring company. And in the nineteenth century the actors offered an escape from the respectability of an industrial era. The bohemianism that was ascribed to them excited the imagination of young men who were forced to earn their living in an office. They were extravagant persons in a sober world, thoughtless in a careful one, and fancy clothed them with glamour. There is in Victor Hugo's Choses Vues a passage, touching in its unconscious humour, in which with awe, astonishment and a spark of envy for such wildness, the sensible little man describes a supper party with an actress. For once in his life he felt a devil of a fellow. Good gracious, how the champagne flowed and what luxury, what silver, what tiger-skins, were to be seen in her apartment!

This glory has vanished. The actors have become settled, respectable and well-to-do. It offended them to be thought a race apart and they have done their best to be like everybody else. They have shown themselves to us without their make-up in the broad light of day, and besought us to see for ourselves that they are golfers and tax-payers and thinking men and women. To my mind this is all stuff and nonsense.

I have known a number of actors very well. I have found them good company. Their gift of mimicry, their knack of telling a story, their quick wit, make them often highly entertaining. They are generous, kindly and courageous. But I have never quite been able to look upon them as human beings. I have never succeeded in achieving any intimacy with them. They are like crossword puzzles in which there are no words to fit the clues. The fact is, I suppose, that their personality is made up of the parts they play and that the basis of it is something amorphous. It is a soft, malleable thing that is capable of taking any shape and being painted in any colour. An ingenious writer has suggested that it is not surprising if for so long they were refused burial in consecrated ground because it is preposterous to suppose that they have souls. This is probably an extravagance. They are certainly very interesting. And the novelist, if he is sincere, cannot but acknowledge that there is between him and them a certain affinity: their character, like his, is a harmony that is none too plausible; they are all the persons they can mirror, while he is all the persons he can beget. The writer and the actor represent emotions they do not, at the moment at all events, feel; and standing with one side of themselves outside life portray it for the satisfaction of their creative instincts. Make-believe is their reality, and the public, which is at once their material and their judge, is also their dupe. Because make-believe is their reality they can look upon reality as make-believe.

32

I BEGAN to write plays, as do most young writers, I expect, because it seemed less difficult to set down on paper the things people said than to construct a narrative. Dr. Johnson remarked long ago that it is much more easy to form dialogues than to contrive adventures. Looking through the old note-books in which from eighteen to twenty I wrote down scenes for the plays I had in mind I find the dialogue on the whole easy and probable. The jokes no longer make me smile, but they are said in the words people would have used then. I caught the colloquial note by instinct. But the jokes are few and savage. The themes of my plays were sombre; and they ended in gloom, despair and death. On my first journey to Florence, I took Ghosts with me, and by way of relaxation, for I was seriously studying Dante, translated it into English from a German version in order to acquire a knowledge of technique. I remember that with all my admiration for Ibsen I could not help thinking Pastor Manders a bit of a bore. The Second Mrs. Tanqueray was then running at the St. James's Theatre.

During the next two or three years I finished several curtain-raisers and sent them to various managers. One or two were never returned and since I had no copies were lost; the others I got discouraged over and put away or destroyed. At that time, and for long after, it was much more difficult than it is now for an unknown playwright to get a production. Runs were long, for expenses were small, and a small band of authors, headed by Pinero and Henry Arthur Jones, could be counted upon to provide the principal theatres with a play whenever one was needed. The French stage was still flourishing and adaptations from the French in bowdlerized versions were popular. I got it into my head, I think from the fact that George Moore's Strike at Arlingford was done by the Independent Theatre, that my only chance of being acted was by making a reputation for myself as a novelist. So I put the drama aside and set myself to writing fiction. The reader may think that this methodical fashion of going to work was unbecomingly business-like in a young author. It suggests a matter of fact turn of mind rather than a heaven-sent compulsion to enrich the world with works of art. When I had published a couple of novels and had a volume of short stories ready for the press, I sat down and wrote my first full-length play. It was called A Man of Honour. I sent it to Forbes Robertson, who was then a popular actor, with the reputation of having artistic inclinations, and when he returned it to me after three or four months, to Charles

Frohman. He also returned it. I rewrote it and at last, having by then published two more novels, one of which (Mrs. Craddock) had a considerable success, so that I was beginning to be looked upon as a serious and promising novelist, I sent it to the Stage Society. They accepted it and W. L. Courtney, a member of the committee, liked it well enough to print it in the Fortnightly Review. He had only published one play before, Mrs. Clifford's The Likeness of the Night, so that it was a great honour.

Since the Stage Society was at that time the only organization of its kind, its productions attracted a good deal of attention and my play was treated by the critics as seriously as though it had been put on for a run in an important theatre. The old hacks, with Clement Scott at their head, abused it soundly; the critic of The Sunday Times stated that it showed no sign of any talent for the stage. I have forgotten who he was. But the critics who had succumbed to the influence of Ibsen treated it as a work worthy of consideration. They were sympathetic and encouraging.

I thought I had taken such a step forward that my course from then on would offer no great difficulties. It did not take me long to discover that, beyond learning a good deal about the technique of playwriting, I had achieved nothing. After its two performances my play was dead. My name was known to the small body of people who were interested in the experimental theatre and if I had written suitable plays I have no doubt that the Stage Society would have performed them. But that seemed to me unsatisfactory. During the rehearsals I had come in contact with the people who were interested in the Society and especially with Granville Barker, who played the leading part in my play. The attitude I found there was antagonistic to me. It seemed to me patronizing and narrow. Granville Barker was very young; I was only twenty-eight, and he, I think, was a year younger. He had charm and gaiety and a coltish grace. He was brimming over with other people's ideas. But I felt in him a fear of life which he sought to cheat by contempt of the common herd. It was difficult to find anything he did not despise. He lacked spiritual vitality. I thought that an artist needed more force, more go, more bluntness, more guts, more beef. He had written a play, The Marriage of Ann Leete, which seemed to me anæmic and affected. I liked life and wanted to enjoy it. I wanted to get all I possibly could out of it. I was not satisfied with the appreciation of a small band of intellectuals. I had my doubts about their quality, for I had been to a stupid and rather common little farce that the Stage Society had unaccountably given and had seen its members consumed with laughter. I was not at all certain that there was not a great deal of pose in their concern for the higher drama. I wanted no such audience as this, but the great public. Moreover I was poor. I had no notion of living on a crust in a garret if I could help it. I had found out that money was like a sixth sense without which you could not make the most of the other five.

During the rehearsals of A Man of Honour I had discovered that some scenes of flirtatious badinage in the first act were amusing and I decided that I could write a comedy. I made up my mind to write one now. I called it Loaves and Fishes. Its hero was a worldly, ambitious parson and the story dealt with his courtship of a rich widow, his intrigues to get a bishopric and his final capture of a pretty heiress. No manager would consider it; it was thought impossible that a play that held a clergyman up to ridicule would be tolerated. I came to the conclusion then that my best chance was to write a comedy with a big part for an actress, who, if she liked it, might induce a manager to give the play a trial. I asked myself what sort of part would be likely to appeal to a leading lady, and having made up my mind on this point, wrote Lady Frederick. But its most effective scene, the scene that afterwards made it so successful, was one in which the heroine in order to disillusion a young lover let him come into her dressing-room and discover her without any make-up on her face and with her hair dishevelled. At that distant time make-up was not universal and most women wore false hair. But no actress would consent to let an audience see her in this condition and manager after manager refused it. I made up my mind then to devise a play in which no one could find anything to object to. I wrote Mrs. Dot. It suffered the same fate as the others. The managers thought it too slight. They complained that there was not enough action and Miss Mary Moore, then a popular actress, suggested that I should insert a burglary to make it more exciting. I began to think that I should never be able to write a piece that a leading lady liked well enough to insist on playing and so tried my hand at a man's play. I wrote Jack Straw.

I had been under the impression that the small success I had had with the Stage Society would impress managers in my favour. To my mortification I found that this was not so. In fact my connection with that body prejudiced me with them, for they decided that I could only write gloomy and unprofitable plays. They could not say that my comedies were gloomy; but they felt them vaguely unpleasant and were convinced that they were uncommercial. I should certainly have given up in despair the attempt to get acted, for one rejection of a manuscript has always discouraged me; but fortunately for me Golding Bright thought that my plays were marketable and took them in hand. He submitted them to manager after manager and at last, in 1907, when I had written six full-length pieces, after ten years' waiting, Lady Frederick was produced at the Court Theatre. Three months later Mrs. Dot was being played at the Comedy and Jack Straw at the Vaudeville. In June Lewis Waller put on at the Lyric a play called The Explorer which I had written immediately after The Man of Honour. I had achieved what I wanted.

33

THE FIRST three had long runs. The Explorer was only just not a failure. I did not make a great deal of money, for in those days the takings of a popular play were much less than they are now, and my royalties were small, but

I was at all events relieved from financial anxiety and my future seemed sure. The fact that I had four plays running at once brought me great notoriety and Bernard Partridge drew a cartoon for Punch in which William Shakespeare was shown biting his fingers in front of the boards that advertised my plays. I was much photographed and much interviewed. Distinguished people sought my acquaintance. My success was spectacular and unexpected. I was more relieved than excited. I think I lack the quality of being surprised, and just as in my journeys I have accepted the most curious sights and the most novel circumstances as perfectly ordinary, so that I have had to force myself to notice that they were remarkable, so now I took all this to-do as natural. One evening when I was dining alone at my club a fellow-member, but a stranger to me, was entertaining a guest at the next table to mine; they were going to one of my plays and began to talk of me. The stranger mentioned that I was a member of the club, whereupon his guest said:

"D'you know him at all? I suppose he's about as swollen-headed as he can be."

"Oh, yes, I know him well," answered my fellow member. "He can't get a hat big enough to fit him."

He did me an injustice. I took the success as my due. I was amused at my notoriety, but not impressed by it. The only definite reaction that I can recall of that period was a reflection that occurred to me when I was walking along Panton Street one evening. Passing the Comedy Theatre I happened to look up and saw the clouds lit by the setting sun. I paused to look at the lovely sight and I thought to myself: Thank God, I can look at a sunset now without having to think how to describe it. I meant then never to write another book, but to devote myself for the rest of my life to the drama.

Though the public accepted my plays with enthusiasm, not only in England and America, but on the Continent, critical opinion was by no means unanimous. The more popular organs praised their wit, gaiety and theatrical effectiveness, but found fault with their cynicism;

the more serious critics, on the other hand, fell very foul of them. They found them cheap and trivial. They told me that I had sold my soul to mammon; and the intelligentsia, of which I had been a modest, but respected member, not only turned a cold shoulder on me, that would have been bad enough, but flung me, like Lucifer, headlong into the bottomless pit. I was taken aback and a trifle mortified, but I bore my disgrace with fortitude, for I knew it was not the end of the story. I had desired a certain end and had taken what I thought were the only possible means to attain it; I could only shrug my shoulders if there were people so stupid as not to see that. If I had continued to write plays as bitter as A Man of Honour or as sardonic as Loaves and Fishes I should never have been given the opportunity of producing certain pieces to which not even the most severe have refused praise. The critics accused me of writing down to the public; I did not exactly do that; I had then very high spirits, a facility for amusing dialogue, an eye for a comic situation and a flippant gaiety; there was more in me than that, but this I put away for the time, and wrote my comedies with those sides of myself only that were useful to my purpose. They were designed to please and they achieved their aim.

I had no intention of fizzling out with a passing success and I wrote my next two plays to consolidate my hold on the public. They were a little bolder and, mild and unsophisticated as they must seem now, they were attacked by the more strait-laced for their indecency. One of them, Penelope, must have had some merit, for when it was revived in Berlin twenty years later it filled the theatre for a whole season.

I had by now learnt all that I was ever able to learn of the technique of the drama, and with the exception of The Explorer, which for a reason I saw very clearly had failed to please so well, I had had an uninterrupted series of successes. I thought it time to try my hand at more serious work. I wanted to see what I could do with more complicated subjects, I wanted to make one or two small technical experiments which I thought would be theatrically effective, and I wanted to see how far I could go with the public. I wrote The Tenth Man and Landed Gentry, and finally, after it had been lying in my desk a dozen years, produced Loaves and Fishes. None of them was a failure; none of them was a success. The managers neither made nor lost money on them. Loaves and Fishes failed to have a long run because the public of that day was uneasy at seeing a clergyman made fun of. The play is written somewhat extravagantly, so that it suggests farce rather than comedy, but it has some amusing scenes in it. The others fell between two stools. One portrayed the narrow, hide-bound life of country gentlefolk; the other, the political and financial world; with both of which I had some acquaintance. I knew that I must interest, move and amuse, and I heightened the note. They were neither frankly realistic nor frankly theatrical. My indecision was fatal. The audiences found them rather disagreeable and not quite real. Then I took a rest for two years and at the end of it wrote The Land of Promise. This had been played to crowded houses for some months when the war broke out. I had produced ten plays in seven years. The intelligentsia, having passed judgement, ignored me, but I was securely fixed in the public favour.

34

FROM TIME to time I had a good deal of leisure during the war; at first because the work I was doing took up but part of my day and to write plays was a convenient means of distracting attention from the activities I was engaged in; and later, when, having contracted tuberculosis, I had to lie long in bed, because it was a pleasant way of passing the time. I wrote a series of plays in quick succession. It began with Our Betters, which was written in 1915, and ended with The Constant Wife, which was written in 1927.

Most of these plays were comedies. They are written in the tradition which flourished so brightly in the Restoration Period, which was carried on by Goldsmith and Sheridan, and which, since it has had so long a vogue, may be supposed to have something in it that peculiarly appeals to the English temper. The people who do not like it describe it as artificial comedy and by the epithet foolishly think they condemn it. It is drama not of action, but of conversation. It treats with indulgent cynicism the humours, follies and vices of the world of fashion. It is urbane, sentimental at times, for that is in the English character, and a trifle unreal. It does not preach: sometimes it draws a moral, but with a shrug of the shoulders as if to invite you to lay no too great stress on it. When the busy Monsieur de Voltaire went to see Congreve to discuss the current drama with him, Mr. Congreve pointed out to him that he was a gentleman rather than a dramatist. The interviewer answered: 'If you were nothing but a gentleman I should not have troubled to call upon you.' Monsieur de Voltaire was certainly the wittiest man of his age, but here he showed want of intelligence. Mr. Congreve's remark was profound. It showed that he knew very well that the first person the author of comedy must consider from the standpoint of comedy is himself.

35

I HAD by then made up my mind on many things connected with the drama.

One of the conclusions I had come to was that a prose play was scarcely less ephemeral than a news sheet. The playwright and the journalist need very similar gifts, a quick eye for a good story and a telling point, animation and a vivid way of writing. All the dramatist needs besides is a specific knack. I do not know that anyone has been able to discover what this knack consists of. It cannot be learnt. It can exist without education or culture. It is a faculty that enables the playwright so to put words that they carry across the footlights and to tell a story, as it were stereoscopically, so that it visibly moves before an audience. It is a very rare faculty: that is why dramatists are so much more highly paid than other artists. It has nothing to do with literary ability as we know from the fact that the most distinguished novelists have generally failed lamentably when they have tried to write plays. It is a faculty, like that of being able to play by ear, of no spiritual importance. But without it, though your ideas may be profound, your theme original and your characterisation acute, you will never be able to write a play.

A good deal has been written about the technique of play-writing. I have read most of the books on the subject with interest. The best way of learning how to write a play is to see one of your own produced. That will teach you how to write lines that the actors find easy to say and, if you have an ear, how far you can carry the rhythm of a sentence without losing the spontaneity of conversation. It will show you what sort of speech and what sort of scene are effective. But I think the secret of play-writing can be given in two maxims: stick to the point and whenever you can, cut. The first of these demands a logical mind. Few of us have it. One idea suggests another; it is very pleasant to pursue it, even though it is not directly concerned with the subject. The inclination to digress is human. But the dramatist must avoid it even more strenuously than the saint must avoid sin, for sin may be venial, digression is mortal. The principle is that of direction of interest. It is important in a novel too, but here greater space permits of greater latitude and, just as according to the idealists evil is transformed into the perfect good of the Absolute, so certain digressions may take their necessary part in the development of the main theme. (A very good example of this is the early history of the Elder Zossima in the Brothers Karamazov.) Perhaps I should explain what I mean by direction of interest. It is the method by which an author causes you to concern yourself with the fortunes of certain people under certain conditions and keeps you attached to them till he has reached his solution. If he lets you wander from the main point it is very likely that he will never recapture your attention. It is a psychological trait in human nature that interest is established in the persons whom the playwright introduces at the beginning of his play so firmly that if the interest is then switched off to other persons who enter upon the scene later, a sense of disappointment ensues. The astute dramatist presents his subject as early as possible, and if for theatrical effectiveness he does not introduce his principal characters till later, the conversation of the persons on the stage at the rising of the curtain concentrates the attention of the audience on them so that the delay in their appearance increases the expectation. No one followed this practice more scrupulously than that very competent dramatist William Shakespeare.

It is the difficulty of directing the interest that makes it so hard to write the plays that are known as plays of atmosphere. The best known of them, of course, are Chekov's. Since the interest is not concentrated on two or three persons, but on a group, and since the theme is their relations with one another and the environment, the author must take care to counteract the natural inclination of the audience to concern themselves with one character or two more than with the rest. With the interest thus dispersed it is possible that the audience will not feel warmly about any of the persons of the play, and since the author must beware that none of his threads is more important than the other, and thus attracts more vividly the attention of the audience, every incident must be subdued to the minor key. So it is very difficult to prevent the audience from feeling a certain monotony and because nothing, either incident or character, has been very forcibly impressed upon them they are very likely to take away with them, when the play is over, some confusion of spirit. In practice it has been shown that such plays are only tolerable when they are perfectly acted.

Now I come to my second maxim. However brilliant a scene may be, however witty a line or profound a reflection, if it is not essential to his play the dramatist must cut it. Here it may serve him if he is also a man of letters. The pure dramatist looks upon it as something of a miracle that he should be able to put words on paper at all, and when they are there, out of his own brain, if not straight from heaven, he looks upon them as sacred. He cannot bear to sacrifice one of them. I well remember Henry Arthur Jones showing me one of his manuscripts and my surprise on noticing that he had written such a simple sentence as, will you have sugar in your tea? in three different ways. It is no wonder that people to whom words come so reluctantly should attach an inordinate importance to them. The man of letters is accustomed to writing; he has learnt how to express himself without intolerable labour and so can cut with fortitude. Of course every writer hits now and then upon a thought that seems to him so happy, a repartee that amuses him so much, that to cut it is worse than having a tooth out: it is then that it is well to have engraved on his heart the maxim, if you can, cut.

To do so is now more than ever necessary, for audiences are at once quicker-witted and more impatient than ever before in the history of the theatre. Plays have been written in such and such a way because they satisfied audiences. Audiences in the past seem to have been willing to sit out scenes that were elaborately developed and to listen to speeches in which the characters fully explained themselves. It is very different now, and the difference has been occasioned, I suppose, by the advent of the cinema. To-day, audiences, especially in English-speaking countries, have learnt to see the point of a scene at once and having seen it want to pass on to the next; they catch the gist of a speech in a few words and having caught it, their attention quickly wanders. The author must curb his natural desire to get the full value out of a scene or to let his characters display themselves in ample expression. Indications are enough. They will be seized. His dialogue must be a sort of spoken shorthand. He must cut and cut till he has arrived at the maximum of concentration.

36

A PLAY is the result of a collaboration between the author, the actors, the audience, and, I suppose one must add now, the director. For the moment I will consider the audience. All the best dramatists have written with their eye on it and though they have more often spoken of it with contempt than with good will they have known that they were dependent on it. It is the public that pays, and if it is not pleased with the entertainment that is offered it, stays away. A play does not exist without an audience. Indeed the definition of a play is a piece of writing in dialogue devised to be spoken by actors and heard by an indefinite number of persons. A play written to be read in the study is a form of the novel in dialogue in which the author for some reason of his own (obscure to most of us) has eschewed the ordinary advantages of narrative. A play that does not appeal to an audience may have merits, but it is no more a play than a mule is a horse. (Alas, all of us dramatists from time to time give birth to these unsatisfactory hybrids.) Everyone who has had to do with the theatre knows how strangely audiences affect plays; a matinée audience and an evening audience may see quite different plays. We are told that the Norwegian public looks upon Ibsen's plays as comedies rich in laughter; the English public has never seen anything to laugh at in those harassing dramas. The emotion of the audience, its interest, its laughter, are part of the action of the play. It creates it in the same way as we through our senses from the objective data create the beauty of the sunrise and the peace of the sea. The audience is not the least important actor in the play and if it will not do its allotted share the play falls to pieces. The dramatist then is in the position of a tennis player who is left on the court with nobody to play with.

Now the audience is a very curious animal. It is shrewd rather than intelligent. Its mental capacity is less than that of its most intellectual members. If these were graded from A to Z, decreasing with succeeding letters to the zero of the hysterical shop-girl, I should say its mental capacity would come round about the letter O. It is immensely suggestible; individuals will laugh at a joke they have not seen because others who see it do. It is emotional; but it instinctively resents having its emotions stirred and is always ready to escape with a giggle. It is sentimental; but will only accept sentimentality of its own brand: thus in England it will accept the emotions attached to the concept of home, but the concept of a son's love for his mother only excites its ridicule. It is careless of probability if the situation excites its interest, a trait of which Shakespeare made extravagant use; but jibs at a lack of plausibility. Individuals know that they constantly give way to impulse, but an audience insists that every action must have its cogent reason. Its morality is the average morality of the crowd and it will be sincerely shocked by a sentiment that will offend none of its members taken one by one. It does not think with its brain, but with its solar plexus. It is easily bored. It likes novelty, but a novelty that will fit in with old notions, so that it excites but does not alarm. It likes ideas, so long as they are put in dramatic form, only they must be ideas that it has itself had, but for want of courage has never expressed. It will not play if it is hurt or affronted. Its chief desire is to be assured that the make-believe is real.

In essentials audiences never change, but at different periods and in different countries at the same period they rise to different levels of sophistication. The drama pictures the manners and customs of the day, and in its turn affects them, and as these change minor changes follow both in the trappings of a play and in its themes. The invention of the telephone, for instance, has made many scenes redundant, has quickened the pace of plays and has made it possible to avoid certain improbabilities. Probability is a variable factor. It is merely what the audience is prepared to accept. Often there is no rhyme nor reason for this. People leave compromising letters about or accidentally hear things they are not supposed to hear as often as they did in Elizabethan times and it is merely a convention that rejects such incidents as improbable. But what is more important is that there has been a change of heart among us, owing to changes in civilisation, and so certain themes that dramatists favoured have now fallen into desuetude. We are less revengeful than we were and now a play devoted to revenge would be scarcely plausible. Perhaps because our passions are less strong, perhaps even because the teaching of Christ has at last penetrated our thick heads, we look upon revenge as discreditable. I ventured once to suggest that the liberation of women and their new-won sexual freedom had so altered men's views on the importance of chastity that jealousy was no longer a theme for tragedy, but only for comedy; but this observation was received with so much indignation that I will not enlarge upon it.

37

I HAVE given this little analysis of an audience because he nature of the audience is for the dramatist the most important of the conventions within which he must work. Every artist must accept the conventions of the art which he pursues, but it may be that these are of such a nature as to make the art a minor one. It was a poetic convention in the eighteenth century that enthusiasm was objectionable and that imagination must be curbed by reasonableness; so it was only minor poetry that was produced. Now, the fact that the general mentality of an audience is so very much lower than that of its more intellectual members is a factor that the author must deal with. I think it definitely reduces prose drama to a minor place. It has been noticed over and over again that, intellectually, the theatre is thirty years behind the times, and the intelligent owing to its poverty of thought have largely ceased to frequent it. I have a notion that when the intelligent look for thought in a playhouse, they show less intelligence than one would have expected of them. Thought is a private thing. It is the offspring of reason. It depends on the mental capacity of the individual and on his education. Its communication is private from the mind that conceives it to the mind that is prepared to receive it, and if one man's meat is another man's poison, still more is one man's thought another man's truism. But an audience is affected by mass suggestion and mass suggestion is excited by emotion. I have hazarded the opinion that if you classified the members of an audience from A to Z, starting, say, with the critic of The Times and ending with the girl who sells sweet-stuffs in a shop off the Tottenham Court Road, its mental capacity would stand about the letter O. How can you write a play of which the ideas are so significant that they will make the critic of The Times sit up in his stall and at the same time induce the shop-girl in the gallery to forget the young man who is holding her hand? The only ideas that can affect them when they are welded together in that unity which is an audience, are those commonplace, fundamental ideas that are almost feelings. These, the root ideas of poetry, are love, death and the destiny of man. It is not any sort of dramatist who can find anything to say about them that has not been said a thousand times already; the great truths are too important to be new.

Besides, ideas do not grow on a gooseberry bush and few people in a generation can devise new ones. It is very unlikely that the dramatist who is lucky enough to have been born with the faculty of putting things so that they carry across the footlights will also be an original thinker. He would not be a dramatist if his mind did not work in the concrete. He has a quick eye for the instance; there is no reason to expect that he will have a faculty for conceptual thinking. He may have a meditative cast of mind and be interested in the speculations of his time, but there is a long way between this and having the power of creative thought. It might be very well if dramatists were philosophers, but in point of fact they are as little likely to be so as are kings. The only two dramatists in our time who have made their mark as thinkers are Ibsen and Shaw. Both were fortunate in the time of their appearance. Ibsen's advent coincided with the movement for the liberation of women from the inferior position in which they had so long stood; Shaw's with the revolt of youth from the conventionality of the Victorian epoch and the trammels that age had set upon it. They had to their hands subjects new to the theatre that could be displayed with dramatic effectiveness. Shaw had the advantage, useful to any dramatist, of high spirits, rollicking humour, wit and fertility of comic invention. Ibsen as we know had a meagre power of invention; his characters under different names are very dully repeated and his intrigue from play to play is little varied. It is not a gross exaggeration to say that his only gambit is the sudden arrival of a stranger who comes into a stuffy room and opens the windows; whereupon the people who were sitting there catch their death of cold and everything ends unhappily. When you consider the mental content of what these authors had to offer, you can, unless you are but ill educated, hardly fail to see that it consisted of no more than the common culture of the day. Shaw's ideas were expressed with great vivacity. They could only have surprised because the intellectual capacity of the audience was inconsiderable. They surprise no longer; indeed, the young tend to look on them now as antiquated buffooneries. The disadvantage of ideas in the theatre is that if they are acceptable, they are accepted and so kill the play that helped to diffuse them. For nothing is so tiresome in the theatre as to be forced to listen to the exposition of ideas that you are willing to take for granted. Now that everyone admits the right of a woman to her own personality it is impossible to listen to A Doll's House without impatience. The dramatist of ideas loads the dice against himself. Plays are ephemeral enough in any case, because they must be dressed in the fashion of the moment and fashions change so that they lose the actuality which is one of their attractive features; it seems a pity to make them more ephemeral still by founding them on ideas that will be stale the day after to-morrow. When I say that plays are ephemeral, I am of course not speaking of plays in verse; the greatest and noblest of the arts can lend its own life to the humble partner; I am speaking of the plays in prose with which our modern theatre is alone occupied. I can think of no serious prose play that has survived the generation that gave it birth. A few comedies have haphazardly travelled down a couple of centuries or so. They are revived now and then because a famous part tempts a leading actor, or a manager in want of a stop-gap thinks he will put on a play on which he has no royalties to pay. They are museum pieces. The audience laughs at their wit with politeness and at their farce with embarrassment. They are not held nor taken out of themselves. They cannot believe and so are never caught by the illusion of the theatre.

But if a play is naturally ephemeral why, the dramatist may ask, should he not look upon himself as a journalist, a journalist of the better class who writes for the sixpenny weeklies, and produce plays on the current topics, political and social, of the day? His ideas will be neither more nor less original than those of the serious young men who write in these journals. There is no reason why they should be less interesting; and if by the time the play has run its course they are out of date, what of it? The play is dead anyway. Now to this question the answer is that there is no reason at all, if he can get away with it and if he thinks it worth while. But he must be warned that he will get little thanks from the critics. For though they clamour for the play of ideas, when he presents it to them they sniff at it if the ideas are familiar to them, thinking modestly that what they know already is commonplace, and if the ideas are unfamiliar to them, they think them perfect nonsense and come down on him like a thousand of bricks. Even the licensed Shaw has not escaped the horns of this dilemma.

Societies have been founded in order to produce plays that people may go to who disdain the commercial theatre. They languish. The intelligentsia cannot be persuaded to patronise these performances, and if they do, want to go without paying. There are a number of dramatists who spend their whole careers writing plays which are only produced by these societies. They are trying to do something for which the drama is unsuited; once they have got a number of persons into the playhouse, these become an audience, and then, even though their average mentality is higher than the ordinary, they are subject to the reactions by which an audience is governed. They are swayed by emotion rather than by reasoning. They demand action rather than debate. (By action of course I do not mean merely physical action: from the standpoint of the theatre a character who says, I have a headache, performs an action as much as one who falls off a steeple.) When the plays these authors write fail, they claim it is because audiences have not the sense to appreciate them. I do not think they are right. Their plays fail because they have no dramatic value. Let no one think that commercial plays succeed because they are bad plays. The story they tell may be hackneyed, the dialogue commonplace and the characterisation ordinary, they succeed notwithstanding because they have the essential, though doubtless trivial, merit of holding their audiences by the specific appeal of drama. But that this need not be the only merit of the commercial play is shown by those of Lope de Vega, Shakespeare and Molière.

38

IF I have thus enlarged on the play of ideas, it is because I think the demand for it is responsible for the lamentable decadence of our theatre. The critics clamour for them. Now, the critics are of necessity the worst judges of plays. For consider, the play appeals to the audience as a unity, the current that passes infectiously from one person to another is essential to the dramatist; he wants to excite a contagion; he must take people out of themselves so that they become an instrument for him to play on, and what they give back, the resonance, the tone, the emotion, is part of his play. But the critic is there not to feel but to judge. He must hold aloof from the contagion that has captured the group and keep his selfpossession. He must not allow his heart to carry him away; his head must remain well screwed on his shoulders. He must take care not to become part of the audience. He is not there to play his part in the play, but to watch it from the outside. The result is that he does not see the play they see because he has not, as they have, acted in it. It is natural enough then that he should ask for different things in a play from those the audience asks for.

There is no reason why he should get it. Plays are not written for critics. Or at least, they should not be. But playwrights are sensitive creatures, and when they are told that the plays they write are an insult to the adult intelligence, they are distressed. They would like to do better, and so the young, aspiring ones, still trailing clouds of glory, sit down to write plays of ideas. That it can be done, and bring fame and fortune, the example of Bernard Shaw is there to show them.

The influence of Shaw on the English stage of to-day has been devastating. The public have not always liked his plays, any more than they liked Ibsen's, but after seeing them they have liked those written according to the old conventions even less. Disciples arose who sought to follow in his steps, but the event has proved that it was impossible to do so without his great gifts. The most talented of these was Granville Barker. As many scenes in his plays show, Granville Barker had it in him to be a very good playwright; he had a dramatic gift, facility for writing easy, natural and amusing dialogue, and an eye for theatrically effective character. The influence of Shaw led him to attach importance to ideas that were somewhat commonplace and to suppose that the natural discursiveness of his mind was a virtue. If he had not been persuaded that the public were fools, who must be bullied rather than cajoled, he would by the usual method of trial and error have learnt to correct his faults, and then might have added to the drama of this country a number of popular plays of great excellence. The lesser followers of Bernard Shaw have only copied his defects. Shaw has succeeded on the stage not because he is a dramatist of ideas, but because he is a dramatist. But he is inimitable. He owes his originality to an idiosyncrasy, not of course peculiar to himself, that had never before found expression on the stage. The English, whatever they were in the Elizabethan era, are not an amorous race. Love with them is more sentimental than passionate. They are of course sufficiently sexual for the purpose of reproducing their species, but they cannot control the instinctive feeling that the sexual act is disgusting. They are more inclined to look upon love as affection or benevolence than as passion. They regard with approval its sublimations which dons describe in scholarly books, and with repulsion or with ridicule its frank expression. English is the only modern language in which it has been found necessary to borrow from the Latin a word with a depreciatory meaning, the word uxorious, for a man's devoted love for his wife. That love should absorb a man has seemed to them unworthy. In France a man who has ruined himself for women is generally regarded with sympathy and admiration; there is a feeling that it was worth while, and the man who has done it feels even a certain pride in the fact; in England he will be thought and will think himself a damned fool. That is why Antony and Cleopatra has always been the least popular of Shakespeare's greater plays. Audiences have felt that it was contemptible to throw away an empire for a woman's sake. Indeed if it were not founded on an accepted legend they would be unanimous in asserting that such a thing was incredible.

To audiences who had been forced to sit through plays in which love was the motive of the intrigue, but who had an instinctive feeling that love, though all very well in its way, was not really quite so important as the dramatists pretended, for after all there were politics, golf, getting on with one's job and all sorts of other things, it was a welcome relief to come upon a dramatist for whom love was a tiresome, secondary business, a quick gratification of a momentary impulse whose consequences were generally awkward. Though put as things must be put on the stage in an exaggerated way (and it should never be forgotten that Shaw is an extremely skilful dramatist) there was enough truth in this attitude to impress. It responded to the deep-seated puritanism of the Anglo-Saxon race. But, if not amorous, the English are sentimental and emotional, and they felt that it was not the whole truth. When other dramatists repeated it, not because it was, as with Shaw, a natural expression of a personality, but because it was striking and effective, its one-sidedness became tediously apparent. The author describes for you his private world, and if it interests you, you will give him your attention. There is no reason why you should trouble yourself with a description of it at second hand. It is inept to say again what Shaw has said so well.

39

TO MY mind, the drama took a wrong turning when the demand for realism led it to abandon the ornament of verse. Verse has a specific dramatic value as anyone can see by observing in himself the thrilling effect of a tirade in one of Racine's plays or of any of Shakespeare's great set pieces; and this is independent of the sense; it is due to the emotional power of rhythmical speech. But more than that: verse forces on the matter a conventional form that heightens the æsthetic effect. It enables the drama to achieve a beauty that is out of the question in a prose play. However much you may admire The Wild Duck, The Importance of Being Earnest or Man and Superman, you cannot without abuse of the word claim that they are beautiful. But the chief value of verse is that it delivers a play from sober reality. It puts it on another level, at one remove from life, and so makes it easier for the audience to attune themselves to that state of feeling in which they are most susceptible to the drama's specific appeal. In that artificial medium life is not presented in a word-for-word translation, but in a free rendering, and thus the dramatist has ample scope for the effects of which his art is capable. For the drama is make-believe. It does not deal with truth but with effect. That willing suspension of disbelief of which Coleridge wrote is essential to it. The importance of truth to the dramatist is that it adds to interest, but to the dramatist truth is only verisimilitude. It is what he can persuade his audience to accept. If they will believe that a man can doubt his wife's fidelity because someone tells him he has found her handkerchief in somebody else's possession, well and good, that is sufficient motive for his jealousy; if they will believe that a six-course dinner can be eaten in ten minutes, well and good again, the dramatist can get on with his play. But when a greater and greater realism, both in motive and in action, is demanded of him and he is asked not to embroider gaily or romantically upon life but to copy it, he is robbed of a great part of his resources. He is forced to forgo asides because people do not naturally talk to themselves out loud; he may not telescope events, by which he was able to accelerate his action, but must cause them to occur as deliberately as in real life; he must eschew accident and chance, for we know (in the theatre) that things do not happen like that. The result has shown that realism too often can only produce plays that are drab and dull.

When the movies learnt to talk the prose play was powerless to defend itself. The movies could represent action much more effectively, and action is the essence of drama. The screen gave that artificiality which verse had once given to drama so that a different standard of verisimilitude was set and improbability was acceptable if only it gave rise to situation. It gave the opportunity for all manner of novel, picturesque and dramatic effects that stimulated and excited the public. The dramatist of ideas had to swallow the bitter pill that the intelligentsia for which he wrote would have nothing to do with his plays, but roared with laughter at the farce and wallowed in the thrills and spectacle of the moving pictures. The fact was of course that they had succumbed to the atmosphere the stage-play had taken pains to lose and were delivered to the sway of make-believe that had held the audiences who first saw the plays of Lope de Vega and William Shakespeare.

I have always eschewed the prophetic role and have left to others the reformation of my fellows, but I cannot but state my belief that the prose drama to which I have given so much of my life will soon be dead. The minor arts, which depend on the manners and customs of the time rather than on deep-seated human necessities, come and go. The madrigal which was once a popular form of musical entertainment, exciting composers to write for it and producing an elaborate school of performers, succumbed when musical intruments were invented that produced more beautifully the peculiar effects it sought; and there is no reason why prose drama should not suffer the same fate. It may be said that the screen can never give exactly the sympathetic thrill you feel when you see living persons in flesh and blood before you. It might very well have been said that strings and wood could never make up for the intimate quality of the human voice. The event has proved that they could.

One thing seems certain, and that is that if the stage play has any chance at all of survival, it is not by trying to do any longer what the pictures can do better. Those dramatists have followed a false trail who by a multitude of little scenes have tried to reproduce the rapid action and varied setting of the cinematograph. It has occurred to me that possibly the dramatist would be wise now to go back to the origins of modern drama and call to his aid verse, dancing, music and pageantry so that he might appeal to all possible sources of entertainment; but I am conscious that here again the cinema with its great resources can do better whatever the spoken theatre can do; and of course a play of this kind would need a dramatist who was also a poet. Perhaps the best chance the realistic dramatist has to-day is to occupy himself with what, till now at all events, the screen has not succeeded very well in presenting—the drama in which the action is inner rather than outer and the comedy of wit. The screen demands physical action. Emotion which cannot be translated into this, and the humour whose appeal is mental, have little value for it. It may be that, for some time at all events, such plays would have their appeal.

But so far as comedy is concerned, it should be recognized that the demand for realism is unjustified. Comedy is an artificial thing and so only the appearance, not the reality, of naturalism is in place. The laugh must be sought for its own sake. The playwright's aim is not now to represent life as it is (a tragic business) but to comment on it satirically and amusingly. The audience should not be allowed to ask, do such things happen?

They should be content to laugh. In comedy more than ever must the playwright exact a willing suspension of disbelief. So the critics are wrong when they complain that a comedy now and then 'degenerates' into farce. It has been found in practice that it is impossible to hold the attention of an audience through three acts of pure comedy. For comedy appeals to the collective mind of the audience and this grows fatigued; while farce appeals to a more robust organ, their collective belly. The great writers of comedy, Shakespeare, Molière and Bernard Shaw, have never jibbed at the farcical. It is the life blood that makes the body of comedy viable.

40

THESE IDEAS floating vaguely in my mind had little by little made me increasingly dissatisfied with the theatre and at last I decided to have done with it. I have never taken very comfortably to collaboration, and as I have pointed out, a play is more than any other artistic product a matter of collective effort. I found it more and more difficult to work in harmony with my collaborators.

It is often said that good actors can get out of a play more than the author has put into it. That is not true. A good actor, bringing to a part his own talent, often gives it a value that the layman on reading the play had not seen in it, but at the utmost he can do no more than reach the ideal that the author has seen in his mind's eye. He has to be an actor of address to do this; for the most part the author has to be satisfied with an approximation to the performance he visualized. In all my plays I have been fortunate enough to have some of the parts acted as I wanted; but in none have I had all the parts so acted. This is obviously inevitable, for the actor who is suited to a certain role may very well be engaged and you have to put up with the second or the third best, because there is no help for it. In recent years, as everyone knows who has had to do with the casting of plays, the competition of New York and of the pictures both in England and America has made it more than ever difficult to get the right person for a certain part; and over and over again a manager finds himself obliged to engage an actor who he knows is mediocre because no one else can be got. Another difficulty is that of salaries. A small part often wants clever playing and so an actor of experience, but from the standpoint of the management it will only stand a certain salary and it is impracticable to engage for it the proper person. The part then is inadequately acted and the balance of the play jeopardized; a scene that has a definite value is thrown away because it is improperly played. It often happens also that the perfect actor for a part will not play it because it is too small or too unsympathetic.

In saying all this, I have no intention of minimizing my obligation to the distinguished actors and actresses to whom is due so much of the success many of my plays have had. My debt to them is great. The list of those who fulfilled all my hopes is so long that it would be tedious to give it, but there is one actor whom, since he has never reached the rank of a star and so has hardly received the recognition that he deserves, I should like to mention. This is C. V. France. He has acted in several of my plays. He has never played a part in which he has not been admirable. He has represented to the smallest particular the character that I had in my mind's eye. It would be difficult to find on the English stage a more competent, intelligent and versatile actor. On the other hand, I have had plays produced in which I was conscious that the audience were not seeing anything like what I wanted them to see. Errors of casting, especially when they occur with actors of reputation, can often not be rectified, and then the author has the mortification of being judged by something that is merely a misrepresentation of his intent. There is no such thing as an actor-proof part. There are effective parts, and parts, often very important ones, that are the reverse, but however effective a part is, it is only fully realized when it is perfectly played. The funniest line in the world is only funny if it is said in the right way; however tender a scene is it will go for nothing if it is played without tenderness. Another pitfall that the actors prepare for the dramatist is one that is not often realized. The system of choosing actors to play themselves makes it very difficult to avoid. An author devises a character, then an actor is chosen because he has the traits the author has indicated; but the addition of his idiosyncrasies to those the author has already given his character results in an absurd exaggeration; the person of the author's invention, who was plausible and natural, is in this way turned into a grotesque. I have often sought to cast an actor contrary to his type, but I do not know that the notion has proved successful; it needs a greater adaptability than modern actors have. Probably the dramatist's best way to cope with this difficulty is to underwrite his parts, lightly sketching the characters and counting on the actors to fill them in with their own individualities. But then he must be certain of getting actors who can do this.

Exaggeration of this kind, wrong casting, inevitable sometimes, already sufficiently distort the author's intention and this is too often further distorted by the director. When I first began to write for the stage, directors took a more modest view of their functions than they have lately done. Then they confined themselves to cutting where the author had been long-winded and disguising by their ingenuity his errors of construction; they arranged the positions of the actors and helped them to get the best out of their parts. I think it must have been Reinhardt who first exacted for the director a preponderating share in the collaboration. His example was followed by directors who lacked his talent and more than once since the preposterous claim has been made that the author's script is to be looked upon merely as a vehicle for the director to express his own ideas. Instances have been known of directors who imagined that they were playwrights. Gerald du Maurier, a very good director, told me himself that he took no interest in directing a play that he could not partly rewrite. This was an extreme case. But it has certainly become very hard to find a director who is content to interpret his author's play; he has too often come to look upon it as an opportunity for an original creation of his own. The public would be surprised if they knew how often an author's purport is misrepresented by the director's stupid obstinacy and how much vulgarity and silliness for which they blame him is due to the director. The director is a man of ideas, but of few, and that is a disastrous thing. To conceive ideas is exhilarating, but it is only safe when you conceive so many that you ascribe no undue consequence to them and can take them for what they are worth. People who conceive few find it very difficult not to regard them with inordinate respect. A director who thinks of a scrap of dialogue, a bit of business or a scenic effect, will attach so much importance to it that he will cheerfully hang up the action of the play or distort its meaning in order to introduce it. Too often the director is vain, self-opinionated and unimaginative; he is sometimes so autocratic that he will force the cast to reproduce his own intonations and his own mannerisms; the actors, dependent on his good word to get parts and on their docility to gain his favour, can but slavishly do as they are told, thus taking all spontaneity from their performance. The best director is the one who does least. I have been lucky enough now and then to be given directors who were honestly anxious to do their best by the play and who have tried to fulfil my wishes; but it is very difficult to enter into somebody else's mind and the most sympathetic director can hardly do more than give an adumbration of the author's intention. I think he often gives the audience something that they like more than they would have liked what the author meant. But that is not to the author's purpose.

The remedy of course is for the author to direct his own play. Few can but those who have themselves been actors. It is not enough to be able to tell an actor that an intonation or a gesture is wrong, you must be able to show him by word and deed what is right. This is more than ever necessary now that the players of minor parts (have an inadequate technique. Gerald du Maurier used often to do this by the mortifying, but efficacious, expedient of caricaturing the manner in which an actor had done something and then showing him how it should be done. He could do this only because he was a very good mimic and a very good actor. But this is a small matter. Direction is a complicated affair. It is a business, or if you like an art, of its own that has to be acquired with pains. The director deals with the mechanics of the play, the entrances and exits, the positions assigned to various characters so that their grouping may be seemly and that they may be so placed that at the proper time the attention of the audience is easily turned on them; he takes into consideration the peculiarities of individual actors and when one is asked to do something that is not within his powers by subterfuge gets over the difficulty; he is mindful also of the peculiarities of actors in general, such as that no English player can now say a speech of more than twenty lines without feeling self-conscious, and devises means of overcoming their diffidence; he directs the audience's interest to the main points of the play and lures them by ingenuity to support the necessarily dull passages of exposition and the joins, the introductions to dramatic episodes, that no play can avoid; he takes account of the facility with which their attention wanders and by the invention of 'business' holds it at dangerous points; he considers the susceptibilities, the jealousy and vanity of actors and takes care that natural egoism does not disturb the balance of the play; he sees that every part is given its appropriate value and that no actor to make his own more important encroaches on somebody else's. He decides when to go quick and when to go slow; when to emphasize, when to slur; when to play up and when to play down. He deals with the sets and sees that they are suitable and practicable to the action; he chooses the clothes to fit the parts and keeps a close watch on the actresses who would sooner be beautifully than aptly dressed; he concerns himself with lighting. Direction is a business, or an art, that needs technical knowledge of an elaborate order. It needs moreover tact, patience, good humour, firmness and pliability. For myself, I have been well aware that I possessed none of the knowledge and few of the qualities that are needed to direct a play. I was hampered besides by my stammer and by the unfortunate accident that after I had written a play and finally corrected the typescript I could no longer take any great interest in it. I was curious to see how it would act, but when once I had given it over to others, like a bitch who takes no more concern in her puppies when others have handled them, I could no longer look upon it any more as intimately my own. I have been blamed often for yielding too easily to directors and accepting their opinions when they were contrary to my own; the fact is that I have always been inclined to think that others knew better than I; I have never liked rows unless I was in a temper and I am seldom in a temper, and lastly, I did not very much care. What added to my growing distaste for the theatre was not that directors were sometimes incompetent, but that they were necessary at all.

41

AND NOW the audience. It must seem ungracious that I should express anything but gratitude to the public that has given me, if not fame, at least notoriety and a fortune that has enabled me to live in the same style as my father lived in before me. I have travelled; I live in a house with a view of the sea, silent and apart from other habitations, in the middle of a garden, with spacious rooms. I have always thought life too short to do anything for oneself that one can pay others to do for one and I have been rich enough to afford myself the luxury of only doing for myself what I alone can do. I have been able to entertain my friends and to help people whom I wanted to help. All this I owe to the favour of the public. I found myself, notwithstanding, growing more and more impatient with that section of it that makes up the theatrical audience. I have mentioned the fact that from the first I felt a singular embarrassment at witnessing one of my own plays, and this, instead of growing less with each play I produced, as I might have expected, grew greater. The feeling that a mass of people were seeing my plays became a sort of horror of distaste, so that I found myself going out of my way to avoid the street in which the theatre was situated where they were acting one of my plays.

I had long come to the conclusion that there was not much point in a play that was not successful and I thought I knew exactly how to write a successful play. I knew, that is to say, what I could expect from an audience. Without their collaboration I could do nothing and I knew how far their collaboration could go. I found myself increasingly dissatisfied with this. The dramatist must share the prepossessions of his audience, the example of Lope de Vega and Shakespeare is there to prove it, and at his boldest he can do no more than put into words what they from cowardice or laziness have been contented only to feel and not to express. I was tired of giving half a truth because that was all they were prepared to take. I grew tired of the absurdity that admits in conversation all manner of facts that must be denied on the stage. I wearied of the necessity of fitting my theme into a certain compass, drawing it out to an unnecessary length or unduly constricting it because a play to attract had to be of a definite length. I grew bored with trying never to be boring. In fact, I did not want to conform any longer to the necessary conventions of the drama. I suspected that I was out of touch with the taste of the public and to decide the matter went to a number of plays that were drawing the town. I found them tedious. I could not laugh at the jokes that amused the delighted audience and the scenes that moved them to tears left me stone cold. That settled it.

I sighed for the liberty of fiction and I thought with pleasure of the lonely reader who was willing to listen to all I had to say and with whom I could effect an intimacy that I could never hope for in the garish publicity of the theatre. I had known too many dramatists who had survived their popularity. I had seen them pitifully writing their own plays over and over again without an inkling that the times had changed; I had seen others desperately attempting to capture the modern spirit and dismayed when their efforts were treated with derision. I had seen famous authors treated with contumely, when

105

they offered a play to managers who had once pestered them with contracts. I had heard actors' scornful comments on them. I had seen the bewilderment, the consternation, the bitterness with which they realized at last that the public was finished with them. I had heard Arthur Pinero and Henry Arthur Jones, both celebrated in their day, say to me identically the same words, one with a grim, sardonic humour, the other with a puzzled exasperation; the words were: 'They don't want me any more.' I thought I would go while the going was good.

42

BUT I had several plays still in my head. Two or three of these were little more than vague schemes and I was willing enough to let them go, but there were four that were lying pigeon-holed in my fancy all ready to be written, and I knew myself well enough to be aware that they would continue to pester me till I wrote them. I had been thinking of them all for a good many years; I had done nothing about them because I did not think they would please. I have always had a dislike to managers losing money over me, due, I suppose, to my bourgeois instincts, and on the whole they have not. It is generally accepted that it is four to one against a play being profitable to a management; I do not think I am exaggerating when I say that the event has proved that with me it has been four to one on. I wrote these four plays in the order in which I expected them to be increasingly unsuccessful. I did not want to destroy my reputation with the public till I was definitely finished with it. The first two surprised me by having a considerable success. The last two had as little as I expected. I will speak but of one of them, The Sacred Flame, and of this only because in it I tried an experiment that some readers of this book may think interesting enough to merit a few minutes' consideration. I tried in this play to write a more formal dialogue than I had been in the habit of using. I wrote my first full-length play in 1898, my last in 1933. In that time I have seen dialogue change from the turgid, pedantic speech of Pinero, from the elegant artificiality of Oscar Wilde, to the extreme colloquialism of the present day. The demand for realism has inveigled dramatists into a naturalism ever greater and greater, a style that has been cultivated to its utmost limit, as we know, by Noel Coward. Not only is the 'literary' avoided, but actuality has been so much sought after that grammar is eschewed, sentences are broken, for it is said that in ordinary life people speak ungrammatically and in short or unfinished sentences, and a vocabulary has been employed in which only the simplest and most ordinary words are allowed. This dialogue is eked out with shrugs, waves of the hand and grimaces. In thus yielding to the fashion it seems to me that dramatists have gravely handicapped themselves. For this slangy, clipped, broken speech they reproduce is only the speech of a class, the speech of the young, ill-educated well-to-do, who are described in the papers as the smart set. They are the persons who figure in the gossip columns and in the pages of illustrated weeklies. It may be a fact that the English are tongue-tied, but I do not think they are so tongue-tied as we are now asked to believe. There are a great many people, members of the various professions and cultured women, who clothe their thoughts in grammatical, well-chosen language and can say what they want to in the right words, put in the right order, with distinction. The present mode, which forces a judge or an eminent physician to express himself as inadequately as a bar-lounger, grossly misrepresents the truth. It has narrowed the range of character that the dramatist can deal with, for he can only show this by speech, and it is impossible to portray people of any subtlety of mind or intricacy of emotion when his dialogue is but a sort of spoken hieroglyph. He is insensibly led to choose as his characters persons who talk naturally in the way his audience have come to think natural and these inevitably are very simple and obvious. It has restricted his themes since it is hard to deal with the fundamental issues of human life, it is impossible to analyse the complexities of human nature (dramatic subjects both) when you confine yourself to a naturalistic dialogue. It has killed comedy, which depends on verbal wit, which in turn depends on the well-turned phrase. It has thus knocked another nail in the coffin of prose drama.

I thought then that in The Sacred Flame I would try to make my characters speak not the words they would actually have spoken, but in a more formal manner, using the phrases they would have used if they had been able to prepare them beforehand and had known how to put what they wanted to say in exact and well-chosen language. It may be that I did not manage it very well. During rehearsals I found that the actors, no longer used to speeches of this sort, had an uncomfortable feeling that they were delivering a recitation and I had to simplify and break up my sentences. I left enough to give the critics grounds for animadversion, and my dialogue was, in some quarters, blamed because it was 'literary.' I was told that people did not speak like that. I never thought they did. But I did not insist. I was in the position of a man in a rented house, whose lease is expiring; it is not worth his while to make structural alterations. In my last two plays I reverted to the naturalistic dialogue I had hitherto used.

When for days you have been going through a mountain pass, a moment comes when you are sure that after winding round the great mass of rock in front of you, you will come upon the plain; but instead you are faced with another huge crag and the weary trail continues; surely after this you will see the plain; no; the path winds on and another mountain bars your way. And then suddenly it lies before you. Your heart exults; there it stretches wide and sunny; the oppression of the mountains is lifted from your shoulders and with exhilaration you breathe the more spacious air. You have a wonderful sense of freedom. So I felt when I had done with my last play.

I could not tell whether I was free from the theatre for good and all, for the author is the slave of what, for want of a more modest word, I am forced to call his inspiration, and I could not be certain that a theme would not some day occur to me that I could not but write in the form of a play. I hoped not. For I was possessed of a notion which I cannot expect the reader to think other than foolishly arrogant. I had had all the experience that it seemed possible the theatre could give me. I had made as much money as I needed to live in the sort of way that pleased me and to provide for such as had claims on me. I had won a great notoriety and perhaps even a passing fame. I might have been satisfied. But there was one thing more I wanted to achieve and this it seemed to me I could not hope to reach in the drama. Perfection. I looked not at my own plays, of whose faults no one could be more irritably conscious than I, but at the plays that have come down to us from the past. Even the greatest have grave defects. You have to make excuses for them by considering the conventions of the time and the conditions of the stage for which they were written. The great Greek tragedies are so far from us and interpret a civilisation that is now so strange that it is hard to judge them candidly. It has seemed to me that perhaps Antigone came very near perfection. In the modern drama I think no one on occasion approached it more closely than Racine. But at the cost of how many a limitation! It was a cherry stone that he carved with infinite skill. Only idolatry can refuse to see the great shortcomings in the conduct and sometimes in the characterisation of Shakespeare's plays; and this is very comprehensible since, as we know, he sacrificed everything to effective situation. All these plays were written in imperishable verse. When you come to the modern prose drama and look for perfection you will not find it. I suppose it will be admitted that Ibsen is the greatest dramatist the last hundred years have seen. For all the vast merits of his plays, how poverty-stricken was his invention, how repetitive his characters, and how silly, when you go a little below the surface, are too many of his subjects! It looks as though defects of one sort or another were inherent in the art of drama. To get one result you must sacrifice another, so that to write a play perfect in all its particulars, in the interest and significance of its theme, in the subtlety and originality of its characterisation, in the plausibility of its intrigue and in the beauty of its dialogue, is impossible. It seemed to me that in the novel and in the short story perfection had been sometimes achieved, and though I could scarcely hope to reach it, I had a notion that in those mediums I could come nearer to it than I had any chance of doing in the drama.

43

THE FIRST novel I wrote was called Liza of Lambeth. It was accepted by the first publisher to whom I sent it. For some time Fisher Unwin had been bringing out in what he called The Pseudonym Series a number of short novels which had attracted a good deal of attention; among them were those of John Oliver Hobbs. They were thought witty and audacious. They made the author's name and confirmed the prestige of the series. I wrote two short stories which together, I thought, would make a volume of a size suitable for this collection and sent them to Fisher Unwin. After some time he returned them, but with a letter asking me if I had not a novel I could submit to him. This was so great an encouragement that I immediately sat down and wrote one. Since I was working at the hospital all day I could only write in the evening. I used to get home soon after six, read my Star, which I bought at the corner of Lambeth Bridge, and as soon as the table was cleared after an early meal, set to work.

Fisher Unwin was hard on his authors. He took advantage of my youth, my inexperience, and my delight at having a book accepted, to make a contract with me whereby I was to get no royalty at all till he had sold so many copies; but he knew how to push his wares and he sent my novel to a number of influential persons. It was widely, though diversely, reviewed, and Basil Wilberforce, afterwards Archdeacon of Westminster, preached about it in the Abbey. The Senior Obstetric Physician at

St. Thomas's Hospital was sufficiently impressed by it to offer me a minor appointment under him, for soon after it appeared I passed my final examinations; but this, exaggerating its success, and determined to abandon the medical profession, I unwisely refused. A second edition was called for within a month of publication and I had no doubt that I could easily earn my living as a writer. I was somewhat shaken when, a year later, on my return from Seville, I received from Fisher Unwin a cheque for my royalties. It amounted to twenty pounds. If I may judge by its continuing sales Liza of Lambeth is still readable, but any merit it may have is due to the luck I had in being, by my work as a medical student, thrown into contact with a side of life that at that time had been little exploited by novelists. Arthur Morrison with his Tales of Mean Streets and A Child of the Jago had drawn the attention of the public to what were then known as the lower classes and I profited by the interest he had aroused.

I knew nothing about writing. Though for my age I had read a good deal, I had read without discrimination, devouring one after the other books I had heard of to find out what they were about, and though I suppose I got something out of them, it was the novels and short stories of Guy de Maupassant that had most influence on me when I set myself to write. I began to read them when I was sixteen. Whenever I went to Paris I spent my afternoons in the galleries of the Odéon browsing among the books there. A certain number of Maupassant's books had been reissued in little volumes at seventy-five centimes and these I bought; but the others cost three francs fifty, a sum that I could not afford, so I used to take a book out of the shelves and read what I could of it. The attendants in their pale grey smocks took no notice of me and it was often possible when none of them was looking to cut a page and continue the narrative without interruption. Thus I managed to read most of Maupassant before I was twenty. Though he does not enjoy now the reputation he did then it must be admitted that he had great merits. He was lucid and direct, he had a sense of form, and he knew how to get the utmost dramatic value out of the story he had to tell. I cannot but think that he was a better master to follow than the English novelists who at that time influenced the young. In Liza of Lambeth I described without addition or exaggeration the people I had met in the out-patients' department at the Hospital and in the district during my service as an obstetric clerk, the incidents that had struck me when I went from house to house as the work called, or, when I had nothing to do, had seen on my idle saunterings. My lack of imagination (for imagination grows by exercise and contrary to common belief is more powerful in the mature than in the young) obliged me to set down quite straightforwardly what I had seen with my own eyes and heard with my own ears. Such success as the book had was due to a lucky chance. It augured nothing for my future. But this I did not know.

Fisher Unwin pressed me to write another much longer book about the slums. He told me that was what the public wanted from me and prophesied that it would have, now that I had broken the ice, a far greater success than Liza of Lambeth. But this was not in my ideas at all. I was ambitious. I had a feeling, I do not know where I got it, that you must not pursue a success, but fly from it; and I had learnt from the French to set no great store on the *roman régional*. I was no longer interested in the slums once I had written a book about them, and I had indeed already finished a novel of a very different sort. Fisher Unwin must have been dismayed when he received it. It was a novel set in Italy during the Renaissance and it was founded on a story I had read in Machiavelli's History of Florence. I wrote it because of some articles by Andrew Lang that I read on the art of fiction. In one of them he argued, very convincingly to me, that the historical novel was the only one that the young author could hope to write with success. For he could not have sufficient experience of life to write of contemporary manners; history provided him with a story and characters and the romantic fervour of his young blood gave him the dash that was needed for this sort of composition. I know now that this was nonsense. In the first place it is not true that the young author has not sufficient knowledge to write about his contemporaries. I do not suppose one ever in after life knows people so intimately as those with whom one's childhood and early youth have been passed. One's family, the servants with whom so much of a child's life is spent, one's masters at school, other boys and girls—the boy knows a great deal about them. He sees them with directness. Adults discover themselves, consciously and unconsciously, to the very young as they never do to other adults. And the child, the boy, is aware of his environment, the house he lives in, the countryside or the streets of the town, in a detail that he can never realize again when a multitude of past impressions has blurred his sensibilities. The historical novel calls surely for a profound experience of men to create living people out of those persons who with their different manners and different notions at first sight seem so alien to us; and to recreate the past needs not only a vast knowledge but an effort of imagination that is hardly to be expected in the young. I should have said that the truth was exactly contrary to what Andrew Lang said. The novelist should turn to the historical novel towards the end of his career, when thought and the vicissitudes of his own life have brought him knowledge of the world, and when, having for years explored the personalities of people around him, he has acquired an intuition into human nature that will enable him to understand and so to recreate the figures of a past age. I had written my first novel of what I knew, but now, seduced by this bad advice, set to work on a historical romance. I wrote it in Capri, during the long vacation, and such was my ardour that I had myself awakened every morning at six and wrote with perseverance till hunger forced me to break off and have breakfast. I had at least the sense to spend the rest of the morning in the sea.

44

THERE IS no need for me to speak of the novels I wrote during the next few years. One of them, Mrs. Craddock, was not unsuccessful and I have reprinted it in the collected edition of my works. Of the others two were novelisations of plays that I had failed to get produced and for long they lay on my conscience like a discreditable action; I would have given much to suppress them. But I know now that my qualms were unnecessary. Even the greatest authors have written a number of very poor books. Balzac himself left a good many out of the Comédie Humaine, and of those he inserted there are several that only the student troubles to read; the writer can rest assured that the books he would like to forget will be forgotten. I wrote one of these books because I had to have enough money to carry me on for the following year; the other because I was at the time much taken with a young person of extravagant tastes and the gratification of my desires was frustrated by the attentions of more opulent admirers who were able to provide the luxuries that her frivolous soul hankered after. I had nothing much to offer but a serious disposition and a sense of humour. I determined to write a book that would enable me to earn three or four hundred pounds with which I could hold my own with my rivals. For the young person was attractive. But even if you work hard it takes a long time to write a novel; you have to get it published; then publishers do not pay you till many months have elapsed. The result was that by the time I received the money the passion that I had thought would last for ever was extinct and I had no longer the slightest wish to spend it in the way I had intended. I went to Egypt on it.

With these two exceptions the books I wrote during the first ten years after I became a professional writer were the exercises by which I sought to learn my business. For one of the difficulties that beset the professional writer is that he must acquire his craft at the expense of the public. He is constrained to write by the instinct within him and his brain teems with subjects. He has not the skill to cope with them. His experience is narrow. He is crude and he does not know how to make the best of such gifts as he has. And when he has finished his book he must publish it if he can, partly of course to get the money to live on; but also because he does not know what it is like till it is in print, and he can only find out his errors from the opinions of his friends and the criticisms of the reviewers. I have always heard that Guy de Maupassant submitted whatever he wrote to Flaubert and it was not till he had been writing for some years that Flaubert allowed him to publish his first story. As all the world knows it was that little masterpiece called Boule de Suif. But this is an exceptional case. Maupassant had a post in a government office that provided him both with a living and with sufficient leisure to write. There are few people who would have the patience to wait so long before trying their luck with the public and fewer still who can have had the good fortune to find so conscientious and great a writer as Flaubert to direct them. For the most part writers waste in this way subjects that they could have made good use of if they had not treated them till they had a greater knowledge of life and a more intimate acquaintance with the technique of their art. I sometimes wish that I had not had the good fortune to get my first book accepted immediately, for then I should have continued with medicine; I should have got the usual hospital appointments, gone as assistant to general practitioners in various parts of the country, and done locums; I should thus have acquired a mass of valuable experience. If my books had been refused one after the other I should have come before the public at last with work less imperfect. I regret that I had no one to guide me; I might have been spared much misdirected effort. I knew a few literary people, not many, for even then I had a feeling that their company, though pleasant enough, was unprofitable to the author, and I was too shy, too arrogant and too diffident, to seek their counsel. I studied the French novelists more than the English, and having got what I was capable of getting from Maupassant, turned to Stendhal, Balzac, the Goncourts, Flaubert and Anatole France.

I tried various experiments. One of them at that time had a certain novelty. The experience of life I was for ever eagerly seeking suggested to me that the novelist's method of taking two or three people, or even a group, and describing their adventures, spiritual and otherwise, as though no one else existed and nothing else was happening in the world, gave a very partial picture of reality. I was myself living in several sets that had no connection with one another, and it occurred to me that it might give a truer picture of life if one could carry on at the same time the various stories, of equal importance, that were enacted during a certain period in different circles. I took a larger number of persons than I had ever sought to cope with before and devised four or five independent stories. They were attached to one another by a very thin thread, an elderly woman who knew at least one person in each group. The book was called The Merry-Go-Round. It was rather absurd because owing to the influence on me of the æsthetic school of the nineties I made everyone incredibly beautiful, and it was written in a tight and affected manner. But its chief defect was that it lacked the continuous line that directs the reader's interest; the stories were not after all of equal importance and it was tiresome to divert one's attention from one set of people to another. I failed from my ignorance of the very simple device of seeing the diverse events and the characters that took part in them through the eyes of a single person. It is a device which of course the autobiographical novel has used for centuries, but which Henry James has very usefully developed. By the simple process of writing *he* for *I* and stepping down from the omniscience of an all-knowing narrator to the imperfect acquaintance of a participator he showed how to give unity and verisimilitude to a story.

45

I HAVE a notion that I was more slow to develop than most writers. Around the years that ended the old century and began the new one I was looked upon as a clever young writer, rather precocious, harsh and somewhat unpleasant, but worth consideration. Though I made little money out of them my books were reviewed at length and conscientiously. But when I compare my early novels with those that are written by young men now I cannot but see that theirs are vastly more accomplished. The ageing writer does well to keep in touch with what the young do and from time to time I read their novels. Girls still in their teens, youths at the university, produce books that seem to me well-written, well-composed and ripe with experience. I do not know whether the young mature sooner than they did forty years ago or whether it is that the art of fiction has in that time so much advanced that it is now as easy to write a good novel as then it was difficult to write even a mediocre one. If one takes the trouble to look through the volumes of The Yellow Book, which at that time seemed the last thing in sophisticated intelligence, it is startling to discover how thoroughly bad the majority of its contributions were. For all their parade these writers were no more than an eddy in a backwater and it is unlikely that the history of English literature will give them more than a passing glance. I shiver a little when I turn those musty pages and ask myself whether in another forty years the bright young things of current letters will appear as jejune as do now their maiden aunts of The Yellow Book.

It was fortunate for me that I suddenly achieved popularity as a dramatist and so was relieved of the necessity of writing a novel once a year to earn my living. I found plays easy to write; the notoriety they brought me was not unpleasing; and they earned for me enough money to enable me to live less straitly than I had been obliged to. I have never had the bohemian trait of being unconcerned for the morrow. I have never liked to borrow money. I have hated to be in debt. Nor has the squalid life had any attraction for me. I was not born in squalid circumstances. As soon as I could afford it I bought a house in Mayfair.

There are people who despise possessions. Of course when they say that it ill becomes the artist thus to cumber himself they may be right, but it is not a view that artists themselves have held. They have never lived from choice in the garrets in which their admirers like to see them. They have much more often ruined themselves by the extravagance with which they conducted themselves. After all they are creatures of imagination and state appeals to them, fine houses, servants to do their bidding, rich carpets, lovely pictures, and sumptuous furniture. Titian and Rubens lived like princes. Pope had his Grotto and his Quincunx and Sir Walter his Gothic Abbotsford. El Greco with his suites of rooms, his musicians to play to him while he ate, his library and his grand clothes, died bankrupt. It is unnatural for the artist to live in a semi-detached villa and eat cottage pie cooked by a maid of all work. It shows, not disinterestedness, but an arid, petty soul. For of course to the artist the luxury with which he likes to surround himself is but a diversion. His house, his grounds, his cars, his pictures, are playthings to amuse his fancy; they are visible tokens of his power; they do not penetrate to his essential aloofness. For myself I can say that, having had every good thing that money can buy—an experience like another—I could part without a pang with every possession I have. We live in uncertain times and our all may yet be taken from us. With enough plain food to satisfy my small appetite, a room to myself, books from a public library, pens and paper, I should regret nothing. I was glad to earn a great deal of money as a dramatist. It gave me liberty. I was careful with it because I did not want ever again to be in a position when for want of it I could not do anything I had really a mind to.

46

I AM a writer as I might have been a doctor or a lawyer. It is so pleasant a profession that it is not surprising if a vast number of persons adopt it who have no qualifications for it. It is exciting and various. The writer is free to work in whatever place and at whatever time he chooses; he is free to idle if he feels ill or dispirited. But it is a profession that has disadvantages. One is that though the whole world, with everyone in it and all its sights and events, is your material, you yourself can only deal with what corresponds to some secret spring in your own nature. The mine is incalculably rich, but each one of us can get from it only a definite amount of ore. Thus in the midst of plenty the writer may starve to death. His material fails him and we say that he has written himself out. I think there are few writers who are not haunted by the fear of this. Another disadvantage is that the professional writer must please. Unless a sufficient number of persons can be found to read him he will starve. Sometimes the stress of circumstances is too great for him and with rage in his heart he yields to the demand of the public. One must not expect too much of human nature and an occasional pot-boiler may be accepted from him with lenity. The writers who are in independent circumstances should sympathize with, rather than sneer at, those of their brethren whom hard necessity sometimes forces to do hack work. One of the minor sages of Chelsea has remarked that the writer who wrote for money did not write for him. He has said a good many wise things (as indeed a sage should) but this was a very silly one; for the reader has nothing to do with the motive for which the author writes. He is only concerned with the result. Many writers need the spur of necessity to write at all (Samuel Johnson was one of them), but they do not write for money. It would be foolish of them if they did, for there are few avocations in which with equal ability and industry you cannot earn more money than by writing. Most of the great portraits of the world have been painted because their painters were paid to do them. In painting as in writing the excitement of the work is such that when it is once started the artist is absorbed in doing it as well as he can. But just as the painter will not get commissions unless on the whole he satisfies his patrons, so the writer's books will not be read unless on the whole they interest his readers. Yet there is in writers a feeling that the public ought to like what they write and if their books do not sell the fault is not with them but with the public. I have never met an author who admitted that people did not buy his book because it was dull. There are many instances of artists whose work for long has been little appreciated and who yet in the end achieved fame. We do not, however, hear of those whose work has continued to be ignored. Their number is far greater. Where are the votive offerings of those who perished? If it is true that talent consists in a certain facility combined with a peculiar outlook on the world it is very understandable that originality should not at first be welcomed. In this perpetually changing world people are suspicious of novelty and it takes them some time before they can accustom themselves to it. A writer with an idiosyncrasy has to find little by little the people to whom it appeals. Not only does it take him time to be himself, for the young are themselves only with timidity, but it takes him time to convince that body of persons, whom he will eventually rather pompously call his public, that he has something to give them that they want. The more individual he is the harder will he find it to achieve this and the longer will it take him to earn his living. Nor can he be sure that the result will be lasting, for it may be that with all his individuality he has but one or two things to give and then he will soon sink back into the obscurity from which he difficultly emerged.

It is easy to say that the writer should have an occupation that provides him with his bread and butter and write in such leisure as this occupation affords him. This course, indeed, was forced upon him very generally in the past, when the author, however distinguished and popular, could not earn enough money by writing to keep body and soul together. It is forced upon him still in countries with a small reading public; he must eke out his livelihood by work in an office, preferably under the government, or by journalism. But the English-speaking writer has the potentiality of such an enormous public that writing can very reasonably be adopted as a profession. It would be more overcrowded than it is if in English-speaking countries the cultivation of the arts were not slightly despised. There is a healthy feeling that to write or to paint is not a man's work, and the social force of this keeps many from entering the ranks. You have to have a very decided urge to enter a profession which exposes you to at least a small degree of moral obloquy. In France and in Germany writing is an honourable occupation, and so is adopted with the consent of parents even though its financial rewards are unsatisfactory. You can often run across a German mother who, when you ask her what her young son is going to be, will answer with complacency, a poet; and in France the family of a girl with a large *dot* will look upon her marriage with a young novelist of talent as a suitable alliance.

But the author does not only write when he is at his desk; he writes all day long, when he is thinking, when he is reading, when he is experiencing; everything he sees and feels is significant to his purpose and, consciously or unconsciously, he is for ever storing and making over his impressions. He cannot give an undivided attention to any other calling. He will not follow it to his own satisfaction or that of his employers. The most common one for him to adopt is journalism, because it seems to have a closer connection with his proper work. It is the most dangerous. There is an impersonality in a newspaper, that insensibly affects the writer. People who write much for the press seem to lose the faculty of seeing things for themselves; they see them from a generalized standpoint, vividly often, sometimes with hectic brightness, yet never with that idiosyncrasy which may give only a partial picture of the facts, but is suffused by the personality of the observer. The press, in fact, kills the individuality of those who write for it. Nor is reviewing less harmful; the writer has not the time to read any books but those that directly concern him, and this reading of hundreds of books haphazard, not for the spiritual advantage he may gain from them but to give a reasonably honest account of them, deadens his sensibilities and impedes the free flow of his own imagination. Writing is a whole time job. To write must be the main object of the author's life; that is to say, he must be a professional writer. He is lucky if he has sufficient fortune to make him independent of his earnings, but that does not prevent him from being a professional writer. Swift with his deanery, Wordsworth with his sinecure, were just as much professional writers as Balzac and Dickens.

47

IT IS acknowledged that the technique of painting and of musical composition can only be acquired by assiduous labour, and the productions of dilettantes are rightly regarded with good-humoured or exasperated contempt. We all congratulate ourselves that the radio and the gramophone have driven from our drawing-rooms the amateur pianist and the amateur singer. The technique of writing is no less difficult than that of the other arts and yet, because he can read and write a letter, there is a notion that anyone can write well enough to write a book. Writing seems now the favourite relaxation of the human race. Whole families will take to it as in happier times they entered religious houses. Women will write novels to while away their pregnancies; bored noblemen, axed officers, retired civil servants, fly to the pen as one might fly to the bottle. There is an impression abroad that everyone has it in him to write one book; but if by this is implied a good book the impression is false. It is true that the amateur may sometimes produce a work of merit. By a lucky chance he may have a natural facility for writing well, he may have had experiences that are in themselves interesting, or he may have a charming or quaint personality that his very inexpertness helps him to get down on the printed page. But let him remember that the saying asserts only that everyone has it in him to write one book; it says nothing about a second. The amateur is wise not to try his luck again. His next book is pretty sure to be worthless.

For one of the great differences between the amateur and the professional is that the latter has the capacity to progress. The literature of a country is made not by a few excellent books, I repeat, but by a great body of work, and this can only be produced by professional writers. The literature of those countries that has been produced chiefly by amateurs is thin in comparison with that of the countries in which a number of men, with difficulty trying to make their living, have followed it as a profession. A body of work, an *œuvre*, is the result of long-continued and resolute effort. The author, like other men, learns by the method of trial and error. His early works are tentative; he tries his hand at various subjects and various methods and at the same time develops his character. By a simultaneous process he discovers himself, which is what he has to give, and learns how to display this discovery to the best advantage. Then, in full possession of his faculties, he produces the best of which he is capable. Since writing is a healthy occupation, he will probably go on living long after he has done this, and since by this time writing will have become an ingrained habit he will doubtless continue to produce works of no great consequence. These the public may legitimately neglect. From the standpoint of the reader, very little that the writer produces in the whole course of his life is essential. (By essential, I mean only that small part of him which expresses his individuality, and I attach no implication of absolute value to the word.) But I think he can only give this as the result of a long apprenticeship and at the cost of a good many failures. To do it he must make literature his life's work. He must be a professional author.

48

I HAVE spoken of the disadvantages of the author's profession: now I should like to speak of its dangers.

It is evident that no professional writer can afford only to write when he feels like it. If he waits till he is in the mood, till he has the inspiration as he says, he waits indefinitely and ends by producing little or nothing. The professional writer creates the mood. He has his inspiration too, but he controls and subdues it to his bidding by setting himself regular hours of work. But in time writing becomes a habit, and like the old actor in retirement, who gets restless when the hour arrives at which he has been accustomed to go down to the theatre and make up for the evening performance, the writer itches to get to his pens and paper at the hours at which he has been used to write. Then he writes automatically. Words come easily to him and words suggest ideas. They are old and empty ideas, but his practised hand can turn out an acceptable piece. He goes down to luncheon or goes to bed with the assurance that he has done a good day's work. Every production of an artist should be the expression of an adventure of his soul. This is a counsel of perfection and in an imperfect world a certain indulgence should be bestowed on the professional writer; but this surely is the aim he should keep before him. He does well only to write to liberate his spirit of a subject that he has so long meditated that it burdens him and if he is wise he will take care to write only for the sake of his own peace. Perhaps the simplest way to break the habit of writing is by changing the environment to one that gives no opportunity for the daily task. You cannot write well or much (and I venture the opinion that you cannot write well unless you write much) unless you form a habit; but habits in writing as in life are only useful if they are broken as soon as they cease to be advantageous.

But the greatest danger that besets the professional author is one that unfortunately only a few have to guard against. Success. It is the most difficult thing the writer has to cope with. When after a long and bitter struggle he has at last achieved it he finds that it spreads a snare to entangle and destroy him. Few of us have the determination to avoid its perils. It must be dealt with warily. The common idea that success spoils people by making them vain, egotistic and self-complacent is erroneous; on the contrary it makes them, for the most part, humble, tolerant and kind. Failure makes people bitter and cruel. Success improves the character of the man; it does not always improve the character of the author. It may very well deprive him of that force which has brought him success. His individuality has been formed by his experiences, his struggles, his frustrated hopes, his efforts to adapt himself to a hostile world; it must be very stubborn if it is not modified by the softening influences of success.

Success besides often bears within itself the seed of destruction, for it may very well cut the author off from the material that was its occasion. He enters a new world. He is made much of. He must be almost superhuman if he is not captivated by the notice taken of him by the great and remains insensible to the attentions of beautiful women. He grows accustomed to another way of life, probably more luxurious than that to which he has been used, and to people who have more of the social graces than those with whom he has consorted before. They are more intellectual and their superficial brilliance is engaging. How difficult it is for him then to move freely still in the circles with which he has been familiar and which have given him his subjects! His success has changed him in the eyes of his old associates and they are no longer at home with him. They may look upon him with envy or with admiration, but no longer as one of themselves. The new world into which his success has brought him excites his imagination and he writes about it; but he sees it from the outside and can never so penetrate it as to become a part of it. No better example of this can be given than Arnold Bennett. He never knew anything intimately but the life of the Five Towns in which he had been born and bred, and it was only when he dealt with them that his work had character. When success brought him into the society of literary people, rich men and smart women, and he sought to deal with them, what he wrote was worthless. Success destroyed him.

49

THE WRITER is wise then who is wary of success. He must look with dread on the claims that others make on him because of it, the responsibilities it forces on him, and the hindering activities that it brings in its wake. It can only give him two good things: one, the more important by far, is the freedom to follow his own bent, and the other is confidence in himself. Notwithstanding his pretension and his susceptible vanity the author when he compares his work with what he intended it to be is never free from misgiving. There is so great a distance between what he saw in his mind's eye and the best he has been able to do that for him the result is no more than a make-shift. He may be pleased with a page here or there and regard an episode or a character with approval; I think it must be very seldom that he looks upon any work of his as a whole with complete satisfaction. At the back of his mind is the suspicion that it is not good at all and the praises of the public, even if he is inclined to doubt their value, are a heaven-sent reassurance.

That is why praise is important to him. It is a weakness that he should hanker for it; though perhaps a pardonable one. For the artist should be indifferent to praise and blame, since he is concerned with his work only in its relation to himself, and how it affects the public is a matter in which he is materially perhaps, but not spiritually, concerned. The artist produces for the liberation of his soul. It is his nature to create as it is the nature of water to run down hill. It is not for nothing that artists have called their works the children of their brains and likened the pains of production to the pains of childbirth. It is something like an organic thing that develops, not of course only in their brains, but in their heart, their nerves and their viscera, something that their creative instinct evolves out of the experiences of their soul and their body, and that at last becomes so oppressive that they must rid themselves of it. When this happens they enjoy a sense of liberation and for one delicious moment rest in peace. But unlike human mothers, they lose interest very soon in the child that is born. It is no longer a part of them. It has given them its satisfaction and now their souls are open to a new impregnation.

In the production of his work, the author has fulfilled himself. But that is not to say that it has any value for anyone else. The reader of a book, the observer of a picture, is not concerned with the artist's feelings. The artist has sought release, but the layman seeks for a communication, and he alone can judge whether the communication is valuable to him. To the artist the communication he offers is a by-product. I am not speaking now of those who practise an art to teach; they are propagandists and with them art is a side issue. Artistic creation is a specific activity that is satisfied by its own exercise. The work created may be good art or bad art. That is a matter for the layman to decide. He forms his decision from the æsthetic value of the communication that is offered to him. If it yields escape from the reality of the world he will welcome it, but is very likely at best to describe it only as minor art; if it enriches his soul and enlarges his personality he will rightly describe it as great. But this, I insist, has nothing to do with the artist; it is human that he should be pleased if he has given others pleasure or greater strength; but he should not take it amiss if they find nothing to their purpose in the results of his production. He has already had his reward in the satisfaction of his creative instinct. Now this is no counsel of perfection; it is the only condition on which the artist can work his way towards the unattainable perfection that is his aim. If he is a novelist he uses his experience of people and places, his apprehension of himself, his love and hate, his deepest thoughts, his passing fancies, to draw in one work after another a picture of life. It can never be more than a partial one, but if he is fortunate he will succeed in the end in doing something else; he will draw a complete picture of himself.

At all events to think thus is a consolation when you cast your eye over the publishers' advertisements. When you read those long lists of books and when you discover that reviewers have extolled their wit, profundity, originality and beauty your heart sinks; what chance have you in comparison with so much genius? The publishers will tell you that the average life of a novel is ninety days. It is hard to reconcile yourself to the fact that a book into which you have put, besides your whole self, several months of anxious toil, should be read in three or four hours and after so short a period forgotten. Though it will do him no good, there is no author so small-minded as not to have a secret hope that some part at least of his work will survive him for a generation or two. The belief in posthumous fame is a harmless vanity which often reconciles the artist to the disappointments and failure of his life. How unlikely he is to attain it we see when we look back on the writers who only twenty years ago seemed assured of immortality. Where are their readers now? And with the mass of books that are constantly produced and the ceaseless competition of those that have lived on, how small is the likelihood that work that has been once forgotten will ever be again remembered! There is one very odd, and some may think very unfair, thing about posterity; it seems to choose the works to which it gives attention from those of authors who have been popular in their lifetime. The writers who delight a clique and never reach the great public will never delight posterity, for posterity will never hear about them. It is a consolation to the popular authors who have had it impressed upon them that their popularity was sufficient proof of their worthlessness. It may be that Shakespeare, Scott and Balzac did not write for the minor sage of Chelsea, but it looks as though they did write for after ages. The writer's only safety is to find his satisfaction in his own performance. If he can realize that in the liberation of soul which his work has brought him and in the pleasure of shaping it in such a way as to satisfy to some extent at least his æsthetic sense, he is amply rewarded for his labours, he can afford to be indifferent to the outcome.

50

FOR THE disadvantages and dangers of the author's calling are offset by an advantage so great as to make all its difficulties, disappointments, and maybe hardships, unimportant. It gives him spiritual freedom. To him life is a tragedy and by his gift of creation he enjoys the catharsis, the purging of pity and terror, which Aristotle tells us is the object of art. For his sins and his follies, the unhappiness that befalls him, his unrequited love, his physical defects, illness, privation, his hopes abandoned, his griefs, humiliations, everything is transformed by his power into material and by writing it he can overcome it. Everything is grist to his mill, from the glimpse of a face in the street to a war that convulses the civilized world, from the scent of a rose to the death of a friend. Nothing befalls him that he cannot transmute into a stanza, a song or a story, and having done this be rid of it. The artist is the only free man.

Perhaps that is why the world on the whole has had the profound suspicion of him that we know. It is not sure that he can be trusted when he reacts to the common impulses of men so unaccountably. And indeed the artist, to the indignation of mankind, has never felt himself bound by ordinary standards. Why should he? With men in general the primary end of thought and action is to satisfy their needs and preserve their being; but the artist satisfies his needs and preserves his being by the pursuit of art: their pastime is his grim earnest and so his attitude to life can never be the same as theirs. He creates his own values. Men think him cynical because he does not attach importance to the virtues and is not revolted by the vices that move them. He is not cynical. But what they call virtue and what they call vice are not the sort of things that he takes any particular interest in. They are indifferent elements in the scheme of things out of which he constructs his own freedom. Of course common men are quite right to be indignant with him. But that isn't going to do him any good. He is incorrigible.

51

WHEN, HAVING achieved success as a dramatist, I determined to devote the rest of my life to play-writing I reckoned without my host. I was happy, I was prosperous, I was busy, my head was full of plays that I wanted to write; I do not know whether it was that success did not bring me all I had expected or whether it was a natural reaction from success: I was but just firmly established as a popular playwright when I began to be obsessed by the teeming memories of my past life. The loss of my mother and then the break-up of my home, the wretchedness of my first years at school for which my French childhood had so ill-prepared me and which my stammering made so difficult, the delight of those easy, monotonous and exciting days in Heidelberg, when I first entered upon the intellectual life, the irksomeness of my few years at the hospital and the thrill of London; it all came back to me so pressingly, in my sleep, on my walks, when I was rehearsing plays, when I was at a party, it became such a burden to me that I made up my mind that I could only regain my peace by writing it all down in the form of a novel. I knew it would be a long one and I wanted to be undisturbed, so I refused the contracts managers were anxious to give me and temporarily retired from the stage.

I had written a novel on the same themes when, after taking my medical degrees, I went to Seville. Luckily for me Fisher Unwin refused to give me the hundred pounds I wanted for it and no other publisher would have it at any price; or I should have lost a subject which I was then too young to make proper use of. The manuscript still exists, but I have not looked at it since I corrected the typescript; I have no doubt it is very immature. I was not far enough away from the events I described to see them reasonably and I had not had a number of experiences that later went to enrich the book I finally wrote. It seems to me that if the writing of this first novel did not finally repress into my subconscious the unhappy memories with which it was concerned it is because the writer is not finally disembarrassed of his subject till his work is published. When it is delivered to the public, however heedless the public be, it is his no longer and he is free from the burden that oppressed him. I called my book Beauty from Ashes, which is a quotation from Isaiah, but finding that this title had been recently used, I chose instead the title of one of the books in Spinoza's Ethics and called it Of Human Bondage. It is not an autobiography, but an autobiographical novel; fact and fiction are inextricably mingled; the emotions are my own, but not all the incidents are related as they happened and some of them are transferred to my hero not from my own life but from that of persons with whom I was intimate. The book did for me what I wanted, and when it was issued to the world (a world in the throes of a terrible war and too much concerned with its own sufferings to bother with the adventures of a creature of fiction) I found myself free for ever from those pains and unhappy recollections. I put into it everything I then knew and having at last finished it prepared to make a fresh start.

52

I WAS tired. I was tired not only of the people and thoughts that had so long occupied me; I was tired of the people I lived with and the life I was leading. I felt that I had got all that I was capable of getting out of the world in which I had been moving; my success as a playwright and the luxurious existence it had brought me; the social round, the grand dinners at the houses of the great, the brilliant balls and the week-end parties at country houses; the company of clever and brilliant people, writers, painters, actors; the love affairs I had had and the easy companionship of my friends; the comfortableness and security of life. It was stifling me and I hankered after a different mode of existence and new experiences. But I did not know where to turn for them. I thought of travelling. I was tired of the man I was, and it seemed to me that by a long journey to some far distant country I might renew myself. Russia was very much in the thoughts of people then and I had a mind to go there for a year, learn the language of which I already knew the elements and immerse myself in the emotion and mystery of that vast country. I thought that there perhaps I might find something that would give sustenance and enrichment to my spirit. I was forty. If I meant to marry and have children it was high time I did so and for some time I had amused my imagination with pictures of myself in the married state. There was no one I particularly wanted to marry. It was the condition that attracted me. It seemed a necessary motif in the pattern of life that I had designed, and to my ingenuous fancy (for though no longer young and thinking myself so worldly wise, I was still in many ways incredibly naïve) it offered peace; peace from the disturbance of love affairs, casual it might be in the beginning, but bringing in their train such troublesome complications (for it takes two to make a love affair and a man's meat is too often a woman's poison); peace that would enable me to write all I wanted to write without the loss of precious time or disturbance of mind; peace and a settled and dignified way of life. I sought freedom and thought I could find it in marriage. I conceived these notions when I was still at work on Of Human Bondage, and turning my wishes into fiction, as writers will, towards the end of it I drew a picture of the marriage I should have liked to make. Readers on the whole have found it the least satisfactory part of my book.

But my uncertainties were resolved by an event over which I had no control. The war broke out. A chapter of my life had finished. A new chapter began.

53

I HAD a friend who was a cabinet minister and I wrote and asked him to help me to do something, whereupon I was invited to present myself at the War Office; but fearing that I should be set to clerical work in England and anxious to get out to France at once I joined a unit of ambulance cars. Though I do not think I was less patriotic than another my patriotism was mingled with the excitement the new experience offered me and I began keeping a note-book the moment I landed in France. I kept it till the work got heavy and then at the end of the day I was too tired to do anything but go to bed. I enjoyed the new life I was thrown into and the lack of responsibility. It was a pleasure to me who had never been ordered about since I was at school to be told to do this and that and when it was done to feel that my time was my own. As a writer I had never felt that; I had felt on the contrary that I had not a minute to lose. Now with a clear conscience I wasted long hours at *estaminets* in idle chatter. I liked meeting a host of people, and, though writing no longer, I treasured their peculiarities in my memory. I was never in any particular danger. I was anxious to see how I should feel when exposed to it; I have never thought myself very courageous nor did I think there was any necessity for me to be so. The only occasion upon which I might have examined myself was when in the Grande Place at Ypres a shell blew up a wall against which I had been standing just as I had moved over to get a view of the ruined Cloth Makers Hall from the other side; but I was too much surprised to observe my state of mind.

Later on I joined the Intelligence Department where it looked as though I could be more useful than in somewhat inadequately driving an ambulance. The work appealed both to my sense of romance and my sense of the ridiculous. The methods I was instructed to use in order to foil persons who were following me; the secret interviews with agents in unlikely places; the conveying of messages in a mysterious fashion; the reports smuggled over a frontier; it was all doubtless very necessary but so reminiscent of what was then known as the shilling shocker that for me it took most of its reality away from the war and I could not but look upon it as little more than material that might one day be of use to me. But it was so hackneyed that I doubted whether I should ever be able to profit by it. After a year in Switzerland my work there came to an end. It had entailed a good deal of exposure, the winter was bitter and I had to take journeys across the Lake of Geneva in all weathers. I was in very poor health. There seemed nothing much for me to do at the moment, so I went to America where two of my plays were about to be produced. I wanted to recover my peace of mind shattered through my own foolishness and vanity by occurrences upon which I need not dwell and so made up my mind to go to the South Seas. I had wanted to go ever since as a youth I had read The Ebb-Tide and The Wrecker and I wanted besides to get material for a novel I had long been thinking over based on the life of Paul Gauguin.

I went, looking for beauty and romance and glad to put a great ocean between me and the trouble that harassed me. I found beauty and romance, but I found also something I had never expected. I found a new self. Ever since I left St. Thomas's Hospital I had lived with people who attached value to culture. I had come to think that there was nothing in the world more important than art. I looked for a meaning in the universe and the only one I could find was the beauty that men here and there produced. On the surface my life was varied and exciting; but beneath it was narrow. Now I entered a new world, and all the instinct in me of a novelist went out with exhilaration to absorb the novelty. It was not only the beauty of the islands that took me, Herman Melville and Pierre Loti had prepared me for that, and though it is a different beauty it is not a greater beauty than that of Greece or Southern Italy; nor was it their ramshackle, slightly adventurous, easy life; what excited me was to meet one person after another who was new to me. I was like a naturalist who comes into a country where the fauna are of an unimaginable variety. Some I recognized; they were old types that I had read of and they gave me just the same feeling of delighted surprise that I had once in the Malayan Archipelago when I saw sitting on the branch of a tree a bird that I had never seen before but in a zoo. For the first moment I thought it must have escaped from a cage. Others were strange to me and they thrilled me as Wallace was thrilled when he came upon a new species. I found them easy to get on with. They were of all sorts; indeed, the variety would have been bewildering but that my powers of observation were by now well trained and I found it possible without conscious effort to pigeon-hole each one in my awareness. Few of them had culture. They had learnt life in a different school from mine and had come to different conclusions. They led it on a different plane; I could not, with my sense of humour, go on thinking mine a higher one. It was different. Their lives too formed themselves to the discerning eye into a pattern that had order and finally coherence.

I stepped off my pedestal. It seemed to me that these men had more vitality than those I had known hitherto. They did not burn with a hard, gem-like flame, but with a hot, smoky, consuming fire. They had their own narrownesses. They had their prejudices. They were often dull and stupid. I did not care. They were different. In civilized communities men's idiosyncrasies are mitigated by the necessity of conforming to certain rules of behaviour. Culture is a mask that hides their faces. Here people showed themselves bare. These heterogeneous creatures thrown into a life that had preserved a great deal of its primitiveness had never felt the need to adapt themselves to conventional standards. Their peculiarities had been given opportunity to develop unchecked. In great cities men are like a lot of stones thrown together in a bag; their jagged corners are rubbed off till in the end they are as smooth as marbles. These men had never had their jagged corners rubbed away. They seemed to me nearer to the elementals of human nature than any of the people I had been living with for so long and my heart leapt towards them as it had done years before to the people who filed into the out-patients' room at St. Thomas's. I filled my note-book with brief descriptions of their appearance and their character, and presently, my imagination excited by these multitudinous impressions, from a hint or an incident or a happy invention, stories began to form themselves round certain of the most vivid of them.

54

I RETURNED to America and shortly afterwards was sent on a mission to Petrograd. I was diffident of accepting the post, which seemed to demand capacities that I did not think I possessed; but there seemed to be no one more competent available at the moment and my being a writer was very good 'cover' for what I was asked to do. I was not very well. I still knew enough medicine to guess the meaning of the hæmorrhages I was having. An X-ray photograph showed clearly that I had tuberculosis of the lungs. But I could not miss the opportunity of spending certainly a considerable time in the country of Tolstoi, Dostoievski and Chekov; I had a notion that in the intervals of the work I was being sent to do I could get something for myself that would be of value; so I set my foot hard on the loud pedal of patriotism and persuaded the physician I consulted that under the tragic circumstances of the moment I was taking no undue risk. I set off in high spirits with unlimited money at my disposal and four devoted Czechs to act as liaison officers between me and Professor Masaryk who had under his control in various parts of Russia something like sixty thousand of his compatriots. I was exhilarated by the responsibility of my position. I went as a private agent, who could be disavowed if necessary, with instructions to get in touch with parties hostile to the government and devise a scheme that would keep Russia in the war and prevent the Bolsheviks, supported by the Central Powers, from seizing power. It is not necessary for me to inform the reader that in this I failed lamentably and I do not ask him to believe me when I state that it seems to me at least possible that if I had been sent six months before I might quite well have succeeded. Three months after my arrival in Petrograd the crash came and put an end to all my plans.

I returned to England. I had had some interesting experiences and had got to know fairly well one of the most extraordinary men I have ever met. This was Boris Savinkov, the terrorist who had assassinated Trepov and the Grand Duke Sergius. But I came away disillusioned. The endless talk when action was needed, the vacillations, the apathy when apathy could only result in destruction, the high-flown protestations, the insincerity and half-heartedness that I found everywhere sickened me with Russia and the Russians. I also came back very ill indeed, for in the position I was in I could not profit by the abundant supplies that made it possible for the embassies to serve their countries on a full stomach and I was (like the Russians themselves) reduced to a meagre diet. (When I arrived in Stockholm, where I had a day to wait for the destroyer that was to take me across the North Sea, I went into a confectioner's, bought a pound of chocolates and ate them in the street.) A scheme to send me to Rumania in connection with some Polish intrigue, the details of which I now forget, fell through. I was not sorry, for I was coughing my head off and constant fever made my nights very uncomfortable. I went to see the most eminent specialist I could find in London. He packed me off to a sanatorium in the North of Scotland, Davos and St. Moritz at that time being inconvenient to go to, and for the next two years I led an invalid life.

I had a grand time. I discovered for the first time in my life how very delightful it is to lie in bed. It is astonishing how varied life can be when you stay in bed all day and how much you find to do. I delighted in the privacy of my room with the immense window wide open to the starry winter night. It gave me a delicious sense of security, aloofness and freedom. The silence was enchanting. Infinite space seemed to enter it and my spirit, alone with the stars, seemed capable of any adventure. My imagination was never more nimble; it was like a barque under press of sail scudding before the breeze. The monotonous days, whose only excitement was the books I read and my reflections, passed with inconceivable rapidity. I left my bed with a pang.

It was a strange world that I entered when I grew well enough to mix during part of the day with my fellow-patients. In their different ways these people, some of whom had been in the sanatorium for years, were as singular as any of those I had met in the South Seas. Illness and the queer, sheltered life affected them strangely, twisting, strengthening, deteriorating their character just as in Samoa or Tahiti it was deteriorated, strengthened or twisted by the languorous climate and the alien environment. I think I learnt a good deal about human nature in that sanatorium that otherwise I should never have known.

55

WHEN I recovered from my illness the war was over. I went to China. I went with the feelings of any traveller interested in art and curious to see what he could of the manners of a strange people whose civilisation was of great antiquity; but I went also with the notion that I must surely run across men of various sorts whose acquaintance would enlarge my experience. I did. I filled note-books with descriptions of places and persons and the stories they suggested. I became aware of the specific benefit I was capable of getting from travel; before, it had been only an instinctive feeling. This was freedom of the spirit on the one hand, and on the other, the collection of all manner of persons who might serve my purposes. After that I travelled to many countries. I journeyed over a dozen seas, in liners, in tramps, in schooners; I went by train, by car, by chair, on foot or on horseback. I kept my eyes open for character, oddness and personality. I learnt very quickly when a place promised me something and then I waited till I had got it. Otherwise I passed on. I accepted every experience that came my way. When I could I travelled as comfortably as my ample means allowed, for it seemed to me merely silly to rough it for the sake of roughing it; but I do not think I ever hesitated to do anything because it was uncomfortable or dangerous.

I have never been much of a sight-seer. So much enthusiasm has been expended over the great sights of the world that I can summon up very little when I am confronted with them. I have preferred common things, a wooden house on piles nestling among fruit-trees, the bend of a little bay lined with coconuts, or a group of bamboos by the wayside. My interest has been in men and the lives they led. I am shy of making acquaintance with strangers, but I was fortunate enough to have on my journeys a companion who had an inestimable social gift. He had an amiability of disposition that enabled him in a very short time to make friends with people in ships, clubs, bar-rooms and hotels, so that through him I was able to get into easy contact with an immense number of persons whom otherwise I should have known only from a distance.

I made acquaintance with them with just the degree of intimacy that suited me. It was an intimacy born on their side of ennui or loneliness, that withheld few secrets, but one that separation irrevocably broke. It was close because its limits were settled in advance. Looking back on that long procession I cannot think of anyone who had not something to tell me that I was glad to know. I seemed to myself to develop the sensitiveness of a photographic plate. It did not matter to me if the picture I formed was true; what mattered was that with the help of my imagination I could make of each person I met a plausible harmony. It was the most entrancing game in which I had ever engaged.

One reads that no one exactly resembles anyone else, and that every man is unique, and in a way this is true, but it is a truth easy to exaggerate: in practice men are very much alike. They are divided into comparatively few types. The same circumstances mould them in the same way. Certain characteristics infer certain others. You can, like the palæontologist, reconstruct the animal from a single bone. The 'characters' which have been a popular form of letters since Theophrastus, and the 'humours' of the seventeenth century, prove that men sort themselves into a few marked categories. Indeed this is the foundation of realism, which depends for its attractiveness on recognition. The romantic method turns its attention to the exceptional; the realistic to the usual. The slightly abnormal circumstances in which men live in the countries where life is primitive or the environment alien to them, emphasize their ordinariness so that it gains a character of its own; and when they are in themselves extraordinary, which of course they sometimes are, the want of the usual restraints permits them to develop their kinks with a freedom that in more civilized communities can be but hardly won. Then you have creatures that realism can hardly cope with. I used to stay away till my receptivity was exhausted and I found that when I met people I had no longer the power to make the imaginative effort to give them shape and coherence; then I returned to England to sort out my impressions and rest till I felt my powers of assimilation restored. At last, after seven, I think, of these long journeys I found a certain sameness in people. I met more and more often types that I had met before. They ceased to interest me so much. I concluded that I had come to the end of my capacity for seeing with passion and individuality the people I went so far to find, for I had never doubted that it was I who gave them the idiosyncrasy that I discovered in them, and so I decided that there was no further profit for me in travel. I had twice nearly died of fever, I had been nearly drowned, I had been shot at by bandits. I was glad to resume a more ordered way of life.

I came back from each of my journeys a little different. In my youth I had read a great deal, not because I supposed that it would benefit me, but from curiosity and the desire to learn; I travelled because it amused me, and to get material that would be of use to me: it never occurred to me that my new experiences were having an effect on me, and it was not till long afterwards that I saw how they had formed my character. In contact with all these strange people I lost the smoothness that I had acquired when, leading the humdrum life of a man of letters, I was one of the stones in a bag. I got back my jagged edges. I was at last myself. I ceased to travel because I felt that travel could give me nothing more. I was capable of no new development. I had sloughed the arrogance of culture. My mood was complete acceptance. I asked from nobody more than he could give me. I had learnt toleration. I was pleased with the goodness of my fellows; I was not distressed by their badness. I had acquired independence of spirit. I had learnt to go my own way without bothering with what others thought about it. I demanded freedom for myself and I was prepared to give freedom to others. It is easy to laugh and shrug your shoulders when people act badly to others; it is much more difficult when they act badly to you. I have not found it impossible. The conclusion I came to about men I put into the mouth of a man I met on board ship in the China Seas. 'I'll give you my opinion of the human race in a nutshell, brother,' I made him say. 'Their heart's in the right place, but their head is a thoroughly inefficient organ.'

56

I HAVE always liked to let things simmer in my mind for a long time before setting them down on paper, and it was not till four years after I had made my notes for it that I wrote the first of the stories I had conceived in the South Seas. I had not written short stories for many years. I began my literary career by writing them and my third book was a collection of six. They were not good. After that I tried now and then to write stories for the magazines; my agents pressed me to write humorously, but for this I had no aptitude; I was grim, indignant or satirical. My efforts to satisfy editors and thus earn a little money rarely succeeded. The first story I wrote now was called Rain and it looked for a while as though I should have no better luck with it than with those I had written in my youth, for editor after editor refused it; but I no longer minded and I went on. When I had written six, all of which eventually found their way into magazines, I published them in a book. The success they had was pleasant and unexpected. I liked the form. It was very agreeable to live with the personages of my fancy for two or three weeks and then be done with them. One had no time to grow sick of them as one easily may during the months one has to spend in their company when writing a novel. This sort of story, one of about twelve thousand words, gave me ample room to develop my theme, but forced upon me a concision that my practice as a dramatist had made grateful to me.

It was unlucky for me that I set about writing short stories seriously when the better-class writers in England and America were delivered over to the influence of Chekov. The literary world somewhat lacks balance, and when a fancy takes it, is apt to regard it not as a passing fashion, but as Heaven's first law; and the notion prevailed that anyone who had artistic leanings and wanted to write short stories must write stories like Chekov. Several writers transplanted Russian melancholy, Russian mysticism, Russian fecklessness, Russian despair, Russian futility, Russian infirmity of purpose, to Surrey or Michigan, Brooklyn or Clapham and made quite a reputation for themselves. It must be admitted that Chekov is not hard to imitate. As I know to my cost there are dozens of Russian refugees who do it quite well: to my cost, because they send me their stories so that I may correct the English and then are offended with me when I cannot get vast sums of money for them from American magazines. Chekov was a very good short story writer, but he had his limitations and he very wisely made them the basis of his art. He had no gift for devising a compact, dramatic story, such a story as you could tell with effect over the dinner-table, like L'Héritage or La Parure. As a man, he seems to have been of a cheerful and practical disposition, but as a writer, he was of a depressed melancholic nature that made him turn away with distaste from violent action or exuberance. His humour, often so painful, is the exasperated reaction of a man whose shuddering sensibilities have been rubbed the wrong way. He saw life in a monotone. His people are not sharply individualized. He does not seem to have been much interested in them as persons. Perhaps that is why he is able to give you the feeling that they are all part of one another, strange groping ectoplasms that melt into each other, the sense of the mystery of life and its futility, which give him his unique quality. It is a quality that has escaped his followers.

I do not know if I could ever have written stories in the Chekov manner. I did not want to. I wanted to write stories that proceeded, tightly knit, in an unbroken line from the exposition to the conclusion. I saw the short story as a narrative of a single event, material or spiritual, to which by the elimination of everything that was not essential to its elucidation a dramatic unity could be given. I had no fear of what is technically known as 'the point.' It seemed to me that it was reprehensible only if it was not logical, and I thought that the discredit that had been attached to it was due only to the fact that it had been too often tacked on, merely for effect, without legitimate reason. In short, I preferred to end my short stories with a full-stop rather than with a straggle of dots.

It is this, I imagine, that has led to their being better appreciated in France than in England. Our great novels are shapeless and unwieldy. It has pleased the English to lose themselves in these huge, straggling, intimate works; and this laxity of construction, this haphazard conduct of a rambling story, this wandering in and out of curious characters who have nothing much to do with the theme, have given them a peculiar sense of reality. It is this, however, that has given the French an acute sense of discomfort. The sermons that Henry James preached to the English on form in the novel aroused their interest, but have little affected their practice. The fact is that they are suspicious of form. They find in it a sort of airlessness; its constraint irks them; they feel that when the author has fixed upon his material a wilful shape life has slipped through his fingers. The French critic demands that a piece of fiction should have a beginning, a middle and an end; a theme that is clearly developed to a logical conclusion; and that it should tell you all that is of moment to the point at issue. From the familiarity with Maupassant that I gained at an early age, from my training as a dramatist, and perhaps from personal idiosyncrasy, I have, it may be, acquired a sense of form that is pleasing to the French. At all events they find me neither sentimental nor verbose.

57

IT IS very seldom that life provides the writer with a ready-made story. Facts indeed are often very tiresome. They will give a suggestion that excites the imagination, but then are apt to exercise an authority that is only pernicious. The classic example of this is to be found in Le Rouge et le Noir. This is a very great novel, but it is generally acknowledged that the end is unsatisfactory. The reason is not hard to find. Stendhal got the idea for it from an incident that at the time made a great stir: a young seminarist killed his mistress, was tried and guillotined. But Stendhal put into Julien Sorel, his hero, not only a great deal of himself, but much more of what he would have liked to be and was miserably conscious that he was not; he created one of the most interesting personages of fiction and for fully three quarters of his book made him behave with coherence and probability; but then he found himself forced to return to the facts that had been his inspiration. He could only do this by causing his hero to act incongruously with his character and his intelligence. The shock is so great that you no longer believe, and when you do not believe in a novel you are no longer held. The moral is that you must have the courage to throw your facts overboard if they fail to comply with the logic of your character. I do not know how Stendhal could have ended his novel; but I think it would have been hard to find a more unsatisfactory end than the one he chose.

I have been blamed because I have drawn my characters from living persons, and from criticisms that I have read one might suppose that nobody had ever done this before. That is nonsense. It is the universal custom. From the beginning of literature authors have had originals for their creations. Scholars, I believe, give a name to the rich glutton who served as a model to Petronius for his Trimalchio and Shakespearean students find an original for Mr. Justice Shallow. The very virtuous and upright Scott drew a bitter portrait of his father in one book and a pleasanter one, when the passage of years had softened his asperity, in another. Stendhal, in one of his manuscripts, has written the names of the persons who had suggested his characters; Dickens, as we all know, portrayed his father in Mr. Micawber and Leigh Hunt in Harold Skimpole. Turgenev stated that he could not create a character at all unless as a starting point he could fix his imagination on a living person. I suspect that the writers who deny that they use actual persons deceive themselves (which is not impossible, since you can be a very good novelist without being very intelligent) or deceive us. When they tell the truth and have in fact had no particular person in mind, it will be found, I think, that they owe their characters rather to their memory than to their creative instinct. How many times have we met d'Artagnan, Mrs. Proudie, Archdeacon Grantley, Jane Eyre and Jérome Coignard with other names and in other dress! I should say that the practice of drawing characters from actual models is not only universal but necessary. I do not see why any writer should be ashamed to acknowledge it. As Turgenev said, it is only if you have a definite person in your mind that you can give vitality and idiosyncrasy to your own creation.

I insist that it is a creation. We know very little even of the persons we know most intimately; we do not know them enough to transfer them to the pages of a book and make human beings of them. People are too elusive, too shadowy, to be copied; and they are also too incoherent and contradictory. The writer does not copy his originals; he takes what he wants from them, a few traits that have caught his attention, a turn of mind that has fired his imagination, and therefrom constructs his character. He is not concerned whether it is a truthful likeness; he is concerned only to create a plausible harmony convenient for his own purposes. So different may be the finished product from the original that it must be a common experience of authors to be accused of having drawn a life-like portrait of a certain person when they had in mind someone quite different. Further, it is just chance whether the author chooses his models from persons with whom he is intimately connected or not. It is often enough for him to have caught a glimpse of someone in a tea-shop or chatted with him for a quarter of an hour in a ship's smoking-room. All he needs is that tiny, fertile substratum which he can then build up by means of his experience of life, his knowledge of human nature and his native intuition.

The whole business would be plain-sailing if it were not for the susceptibilities of the persons who serve as models for the author's characters. So colossal is human egotism that people who have met an author are constantly on the look out for portraits of themselves in his works and if they can persuade themselves that such and such a character is drawn from them they are bitterly affronted if it is drawn with any imperfections. Though they will find fault with their friends freely and ridicule their absurdities, their vanity is so outrageous that they cannot reconcile themselves to the fact that they too have faults and absurdities. The matter is made worse for them by their friends who with malicious indignation offer them feigned sympathy for the outrage they have suffered. Of course there is a lot of humbug about it all. I do not suppose I am the only author who has been vilified by women who claimed that I had stayed with them and abused their hospitality by writing about them when not only had I not stayed with them, but neither knew nor had ever heard of them. The poor drabs were so vain and their lives so empty that they deliberately identified themselves with a creature of odious character in order in some small circle to give themselves a petty notoriety.

Sometimes the author takes a very commonplace person and from him invents a character who is noble, self-controlled and courageous. He has seen in that person a significance that had escaped those he lived with.

Then oddly enough the original goes unrecognized; it is only when you shew somebody with faults or ridiculous foibles that a name is at once assigned. I have been forced to conclude from this that we know our friends by their defects rather than by their merits. The author seldom has the wish to give offence and he uses what means he can to protect his originals; he puts the persons of his invention in different places, gives them another means of livelihood, situates them perhaps in a different class; what he cannot so easily do is to change their appearance. The physical traits of a man influence his character and contrariwise his character is expressed, at least in the rough, in his appearance. You cannot make a tall man short and otherwise keep him the same. A man's height gives him a different outlook on his environment and so changes his character. Nor to cover your tracks can you make a little brunette into a massive blonde. You have to leave them very much as they are or you will lose what it was that moved you to draw a character from them. But no one has the right to take a character in a book and say, this is meant for me. All he may say is, I provided the suggestion for this character. If he has any common sense he will be interested rather than vexed; and the author's inventiveness and intuition may suggest to him things about himself that it is useful for him to know.

58

I HAVE no illusions about my literary position. There are but two important critics in my own country who have troubled to take me seriously and when clever young men write essays about contemporary fiction they never think of considering me. I do not resent it. It is very natural. I have never been a propagandist. The reading public has enormously increased during the last thirty years and there is a large mass of ignorant people who want knowledge that can be acquired with little labour. They have thought that they were learning something when they read novels in which the characters delivered their views on the burning topics of the day. A bit of love-making thrown in here and there made the information they were given sufficiently palatable. The novel was regarded as a convenient pulpit for the dissemination of ideas and a good many novelists were willing enough to look upon themselves as leaders of thought. The novels they wrote were journalism rather than fiction. They had a news value. Their disadvantage was that after a little while they were as unreadable as last week's paper. But the demand of this great new public for knowledge has of late given rise to the production of a number of books in which subjects of common interest, science, education, social welfare and I know not what, are treated in non-technical language. Their success has been very great and has killed the propaganda novel. But it is evident that while its vogue lasted it seemed much more significant and so offered a better subject of discourse than the novel of character or adventure.

The intelligent critics, the more serious novel readers, have since then given most of their attention to the writers who seemed to offer something new in technique, and this is very comprehensible, for the novelties they presented gave a sort of freshness to well-worn material and were a fruitful matter of discussion.

It seems strange that so much attention has been paid to these things. The method that Henry James devised and brought to a high degree of perfection of telling his story through the sensibilities of an observer who had some part in its action was an ingenious dodge that gave the dramatic effect he sought in fiction, a verisimilitude grateful to an author much influenced by the French naturalists and a means of getting round some of the difficulties of the novelist who takes up the attitude of an all-seeing and all-wise narrator. What this observer did not know could be left conveniently mysterious. It was, however, only a slight variation from the autobiographical form that has many of the same advantages, and to speak of it as though it were a great æsthetic discovery is somewhat absurd. Of the other experiments that have been made the most important is the use of the stream of thought. Writers have always been attracted by the philosophers who had an emotional value and who were not too hard to understand. They were taken in turn by Schopenhauer, Nietzsche and Bergson. It was inevitable that psychoanalysis should captivate their fancy. It had great possibilities for the novelist. He knew how much he owed to his own subconscious for the best of what he wrote and it was tempting to explore greater depths of character by an imaginative picture of the subconscious of the persons of his invention. It was a clever and amusing trick, but nothing more. When writers, instead of using it as an occasional device for a particular purpose, ironical, dramatic or explanatory, made it the basis of their work it proved tedious. I conjecture that what is useful in this and similar devices will be absorbed into the general technique of fiction, but that the works that introduced them will soon lose their interest. It seems to have escaped the attention of those who have been taken by these curious experiments that the matter treated of in the books in which they are made use of is of an extreme triviality. It almost looks as though their authors had been driven to these contrivances by an uneasy consciousness of their own emptiness. The persons they describe with all this ingenuity are intrinsically uninteresting and the subjects at issue unimportant. This might be expected. For the artist is absorbed by his technique only when his theme is of no pressing interest to him. When he is obsessed by his topic he has not much time over to think of the artfulness of his presentation. So in the seventeenth century the writers, exhausted by the mental effort of the Renaissance and prevented by the tyranny of kings and the domination of the church from occupying themselves with the great issues of life, turned their minds to gongorism, concettism and such-like toys. It may be that the interest that has been taken during recent years in every form of technical experiment in the arts points to the fact that our civilisation is crumbling; the subjects that seemed important to the nineteenth century have lost their interest, and artists do not yet see what the great issues are that will affect the generation who will create the civilisation which is in course of displacing our own.

59

I LOOK upon it as very natural then that the world of letters should have attached no great importance to my work. In the drama I have found myself at home in the traditional moulds. As a writer of fiction I go back, through innumerable generations, to the teller of tales round the fire in the cavern that sheltered neolithic men. I have had some sort of story to tell and it has interested me to tell it. To me it has been a sufficient object in itself. It has been my misfortune that for some time now a story has been despised by the intelligent. I have read a good many books on the art of fiction and all ascribe very small value to the plot. (In passing I should like to say that I cannot understand the sharp distinction some clever theorists make between story and plot. A plot is merely the pattern on which the story is arranged.) From these books you would judge that it is only a hindrance to the intelligent author and a concession that he makes to the stupid demands of the public. Indeed, sometimes you might think that the best novelist is the essayist, and that the only perfect short stories have been written by Charles Lamb and Hazlitt.

But the delight in listening to stories is as natural to human nature as the delight in looking at the dancing and miming out of which drama arose. That it exists unimpaired is shown by the vogue of the detective novel. The most intellectual persons read them, with condescension of course, but they read them, and why, if not because the psychological, the pedagogic, the psychoanalytic novels which alone their minds approve do not give them the satisfaction of this particular need? There are a number of clever writers who, with all sorts of good things in their heads to say and a gift for creating living people, do not know what on earth to do with them when they have created them. They cannot invent a plausible story. Like all writers (and in all writers there is a certain amount of humbug) they make a merit of their limitations and either tell the reader that he can imagine for himself what happens or else berate him for wanting to know. They claim that in life stories are not finished, situations are not rounded off and loose ends are left hanging. This is not always true, for at least death finishes all our stories; but even if it were it would not be a good argument.

For the novelist claims to be an artist and the artist does not copy life, he makes an arrangement out of it to suit his own purposes. Just as the painter thinks with his brush and paints the novelist thinks with his story; his view of life, though he may be unconscious of it, his personality, exist as a series of human actions. When you look back on the art of the past you can hardly fail to notice that artists have seldom attached great value to realism. On the whole they have used nature to make a formal decoration and they have only copied it directly from time to time when their imagination had taken them so far from it that a return was felt necessary. In painting and sculpture it might even be argued that a very close approximation to reality has always announced the decadence of a school. In the sculpture of Phidias you see already the dullness of the Apollo Belvedere and in Raphael's Miracle at Bolsano the vapidity of Bouguereau. Then art can only gain new vigour by forcing on nature a new convention.

But that is by the way.

It is a natural desire in the reader to want to know what happens to the people in whom his interest has been aroused and the plot is the means by which you gratify this desire. A good story is obviously a difficult thing to invent, but its difficulty is a poor reason for despising it. It should have coherence and sufficient probability for the needs of the theme; it should be of a nature to display the development of character, which is the chief concern of fiction at the present day, and it should have completeness, so that when it is finally unfolded no more questions can be asked about the persons who took part in it. It should have like Aristotle's tragedy a beginning, a middle and an end. The chief use of a plot is one that many people do not seem to have noticed. It is a line to direct the reader's interest. That is possibly the most important thing in fiction, for it is by direction of interest that the author carries the reader along from page to page and it is by direction of interest that he induces in him the mood he desires. The author always loads his dice, but he must never let the reader see that he has done so, and by the manipulation of his plot he can engage the reader's attention so that he does not perceive what violence has been done him. I am not writing a technical treatise on the novel, so I need not enumerate the various devices that novelists have used to achieve this. But how efficacious this direction of interest may be and how injurious its neglect is well shown in Sense and Sensibility and in L'Education Sentimentale. Jane Austen leads the reader so firmly along the line of the simple story that he does not stop to reflect that Elinor is a prig, Marianne a fool, and the three men lifeless dummies. Flaubert, aiming at a rigid objectivity, directs the reader's interests so little that he is perfectly indifferent to the fortunes of the various characters. This makes the novel very difficult to read. I cannot think of another that has so many merits and leaves so shadowy an impression.

60

IN MY twenties the critics said I was brutal, in my thirties they said I was flippant, in my forties they said I was cynical, in my fifties they said I was competent, and now in my sixties they say I am superficial. I have gone my way, following the course I had mapped out for myself, and trying with my works to fill out the pattern I looked for. I think authors are unwise who do not read criticisms. It is salutary to train oneself to be no more affected by censure than by praise; for of course it is easy to shrug one's shoulders when one finds oneself described as a genius, but not so easy to be unconcerned when one is treated as a nincompoop. The history of criticism is there to show that contemporary criticism is fallible. It is a nice point to decide how far the author should consider it and how far ignore it. And such is the diversity of opinion that it is very difficult for an author to arrive at any conclusion about his merit. In England there is a natural tendency to despise the novel. The autobiography of an insignificant politician, the life of a royal courtesan will receive serious critical consideration, whereas half a dozen novels will be reviewed in a bunch by a reviewer who is concerned only too often to be amusing at their expense. The fact is simply that the English are more interested in works of information than in works of art. This makes it difficult for the novelist to get from criticisms of his work anything that will be useful to his own development.

It is a great misfortune to English letters that we have not had in this century a critic of the class, say, of Sainte-Beuve, Matthew Arnold or even Brunetière. It is true that he would not have occupied himself much with current literature, and if we may judge by the three I have mentioned, had he done so it would have been of no direct service to contemporary writers. For Sainte-Beuve, as we know, was too envious of a form of success he hankered after, but never achieved, to treat his contemporaries with fairness; and Matthew Arnold's taste was so much at fault when he dealt with French writers of his day that there is no reason to suppose it would have been any better if he had dealt with English ones. Brunetière had no tolerance; he measured writers by hard and fast rules and was incapable of seeing merit in those who had aims with which he did not sympathize. His force of character gave him an influence that his talents did not warrant. But notwithstanding, writers benefit by a critic who is gravely concerned with literature; even if they resent him they may be incited by antagonism to a clearer definition of their own aims. He can provoke in them an excitement that calls them to more conscious effort and his example urges them to take their art with a more intense seriousness.

In one of his dialogues Plato seemingly has tried to

153

show the impossibility of criticism; but in fact he has only shown to what extravagance the Socratic method may sometimes lead. There is one sort of criticism that is evidently futile. This is that which is written by the critic to compensate himself for humiliations he has suffered in his early youth. Criticism affords him a means of regaining his self-esteem. Because at school, unable to adapt himself to the standards of that narrow world, he has been kicked and cuffed, he will when grown up cuff and kick in his turn in order to assuage his wounded feelings. His interest is in his reaction to the work he is considering, not in the reaction it has to him.

There can seldom have been a greater need than now of a critic of authority, for the arts are at sixes and sevens. We see composers telling stories, painters philosophizing, and novelists preaching sermons; we see poets impatient with their own harmony trying to fit with their verse the other harmony of prose, and we see the writers of prose trying to force on it the rhythms of verse. Someone is badly wanted to define once more the characters peculiar to the several arts and to point out to those who go astray that their experiments can lead only to their own confusion. It is too much to expect that anyone may be found who can speak with equal competence in all the arts; but, the demand producing the supply, we may still hope that one of these days a critic will arise to ascend the throne once occupied by Sainte-Beuve and Matthew Arnold. He could do much. I have read lately two or three books in which a claim is made to form an exact science of criticism. They have not convinced me that such a thing is possible. Criticism to my mind is a personal matter, but there is nothing against that if the critic has a great personality. It is dangerous for him to look upon his activity as creative. His business is to guide, to appraise, and to point to new avenues of creation, but if he looks upon himself as creative he will be more occupied with creation, the most enthralling of human activities, than with the functions proper to him. It is perhaps well for him to have written a play, a novel and some verse, for thus as in no other way can he acquire the technique of letters; but he cannot be a great critic unless he has realized that to create is not his affair. One of the reasons why current criticism is so useless is that it is done as a side-issue by creative writers. It is only natural that they should think the sort of thing they do the thing best worth doing. The great critic should have a sympathy as wide as his knowledge is universal. It should be grounded not on a general indifference, such as makes men tolerant of things they care nothing about, but on an active delight in diversity. He must be a psychologist and a physiologist, for he must know how the basic elements of literature are related to the minds and bodies of men; and he must be a philosopher, for from philosophy he will learn serenity, impartiality, and the transitoriness of human things. He must be familiar not only with the literature of his native land. With standards founded on the literature of the past, and studious of contemporary literature in other countries, he will see clearly the trend that literature in its evolution is pursuing and so be enabled profitably to direct that of his own countrymen. He must support himself on tradition, for tradition is the expression of the inevitable idiosyncrasies of a nation's literature, but he must do everything he can to encourage its development in its natural direction. Tradition is a guide and not a jailer. He must have patience, firmness and enthusiasm. Each book he reads should be a new and thrilling adventure; he judges it by the universality of his knowledge and the strength of his character. In fact the great critic must be a great man. He must be great enough to recognize with good-humoured resignation that his work, though so important, can have but an ephemeral value; for his merit is that he responds to the needs of, and points the way to, his own generation. A new generation arises with other needs, a new way stretches before it; he has nothing more to say and is thrown with all his works into the dust-heap.

To spend his life to such an end can only be worth his while if he thinks literature one of the most important of human pursuits.

61

THAT IS a claim that the author has always made and to this he has added another claim: he has asserted that he was not as other men and in consequence not amenable to their rules. Other men have received it with obloquy, derision and contempt. This he has met in different ways according to his idiosyncrasy. Sometimes he has flaunted his difference from what he was inclined to call the common herd by wilful eccentricity and to *épater le bourgeois* has paraded the red waistcoat of Théophile Gautier or, like Gérard de Nerval, led a lobster tied by a pink ribbon down the street; sometimes he has taken an ironic pleasure in pretending to be the same as every one else and with Browning has dressed the poet within him in the likeness of a prosperous banker. It may be that we are all of us a bundle of mutually contradictory selves, but the writer, the artist, is deeply conscious of it. With other men, the life they lead makes one side of them predominant, so that, except perhaps in the depths of the subconscious, it ends by being the whole man. But the painter, the writer, the saint, is always looking in himself for new facets; he is bored at repeating himself and seeks, though it may be without actually knowing it, to prevent himself from becoming one-sided. He never gets the opportunity to grow into a self-consistent, coherent creature.

Other men have been outraged on discovering, as they so often have, the discrepancy between the artist's life and his work. They have not been able to reconcile Beethoven's idealism with his meanness of spirit, Wagner's heavenly rapture with his selfishness and dishonesty, Cervantes' moral obliquity with his tenderness and magnanimity. Sometimes, in their indignation, they have sought to persuade themselves that the work of such men could not possess the value they thought. When it has been brought to their knowledge that great and pure poets had left behind them a large body of obscene verse they have been horrified. They have had an uneasy feeling that the whole thing was a sham. 'What arrant humbugs these people are!' they say. But the point of the writer is that he is not one man but many. It is because he is many that he can create many and the measure of his greatness is the number of selves that he comprises. When he fashions a character that does not carry conviction it is because there is in himself nothing of that person; he has had to fall back on observation, and so has only described, not begotten. The writer does not feel with; he feels in. It is not sympathy that he has, that too often results in sentimentality; he has what the psychologists call empathy. It is because Shakespeare had this to so great a degree that he was at once the most living and the least sentimental of authors. I think Goethe was the first writer to grow conscious of this multiple personality and it troubled him all his life. He was always comparing the writer that he was with the man and he could not quite reconcile the discongruity. But the end of the artist and the end of other men are different, for the end of the artist is production while the end of other men is right action. And so the artist's attitude to life is in a certain way peculiar to himself. The psychologists tell us that with the ordinary man an image is less vivid than a sensation. It is an attenuated experience that serves to give information about objects of sense and in the world of sense is a guide to action. His day-dreams satisfy emotional needs and fulfil desires that in the world of affairs are frustrated. But they are pale shadows of real life and at the back of his mind is the awareness that the demands of the world of sense have another validity. To the writer this is not so. The images, free ideas that throng his mind, are not guides but materials for action. They have all the vividness of sensation. His day-dreams are so significant to him that it is the world of sense that is shadowy and he has to reach out for it by an effort of will. His castles in Spain are no baseless fabric, but real castles that he lives in.

The artist's egoism is outrageous: it must be; he is by nature a solipsist and the world exists only for him to exercise upon it his powers of creation. He partakes of life only with part of him and never feels the common emotions of men with his whole being, for however urgent the necessity he is an observer as well as an actor. It often makes him seem heartless. Women with their shrewd sense are on the guard against him; they are attracted by him, but instinctively feel that they can never completely dominate him, which is their desire, for they know that somehow he escapes them. Has not Goethe, that great lover, himself told us how he composed verses in the arms of his beloved and with singing fingers softly tapped the beat of his hexameters on her shapely back? The artist is ill to live with. He can be perfectly sincere in his creative emotion and yet there is someone else within him who is capable of cocking a snook at its exercise. He is not dependable.

But the gods never make any of their gifts without adding to them a drawback and this multiplicity of the writer that enables him, like the gods, to create human beings prevents him from achieving perfect truth in their creation. Realism is relative. The most realistic writer by the direction of his interest falsifies his creatures. He sees them through his own eyes. He makes them more self-conscious than they really are. He makes them more reflective and more complicated. He throws himself into them, trying to make them ordinary men, but he never quite succeeds; for the peculiarity that gives him his talent and makes him a writer for ever prevents him from knowing exactly what ordinary men are. It is not truth he attains, but merely a transposition of his own personality. And the greater his talent, the more powerful his individuality, the more fantastic is the picture of life he draws. It has sometimes seemed to me that if posterity wants to know what the world of to-day was like it will not go to those writers whose idiosyncrasy has impressed our contemporaries, but to the mediocre ones whose ordinariness has allowed them to describe their surroundings with a greater faithfulness. I do not mention them since, even though they may be assured of the appreciation of after ages, people do not like to be labelled as mediocre. But I think it may be admitted that one gets the impression of a truer picture of life in the novels of Anthony Trollope than in those of Charles Dickens.

62

SOMETIMES THE writer must ask himself whether what he has written has any value except to himself and the question is perhaps urgent now when the world seems, at least to us who live in it, in such a condition of unrest and wretchedness as it has not often been in before. For me the question has had a special import for I have never wished to be nothing but a writer; I have wished to live life completely. I have been uneasily conscious that it was a duty I owed myself to take some part, however small, in the business of the common weal. My natural inclination has been to keep aloof from every kind of public activity and it has been with the greatest reluctance that I have even served on committees formed to effect some aim of passing interest. Thinking that not the whole of life was long enough to learn to write well, I have been unwilling to give to other activities time that I so much needed to achieve the purpose I had in mind. I have never been able intimately to persuade myself that anything else mattered. Notwithstanding, when men in millions are living on the border-line of starvation, when freedom in great parts of the inhabited globe is dying or dead, when a terrible war has been succeeded by years during which happiness has been out of the reach of the great mass of the human race, when men are distraught because they can see no value in life and the hopes that had enabled them for so many centuries to support its misery seem illusory; it is hard not to ask oneself whether it is anything but futility to write plays and stories and novels. The only answer I can think of is that some of us are so made that there is nothing else we can do. We do not write because we want to; we write because we must. There may be other things in the world that more pressingly want doing: we must liberate our souls of the burden of creation. We must go on though Rome burns. Others may despise us because we do not lend a hand with a bucket of water; we cannot help it; we do not know how to handle a bucket. Besides, the conflagration thrills us and charges our mind with phrases.

From time to time, however, writers have engaged in politics. Its effect on them as writers has been injurious. I have not noticed that their counsel has had much influence on the conduct of affairs. The only exception I can recall is Disraeli; but in his case, it is not unfair to say, writing was not an end in itself, but a means to political advancement. At the present day, living as we do in an age of specialisation, I have a notion that on the whole the cobbler does best to stick to his last.

Because I had heard that Dryden had learnt to write English from his study of Tillotson, I read certain passages of this author and I came across a piece that gave me some consolation in this matter. It ran as follows: 'We ought to be glad, when those that are fit for government, and called to it, are willing to take the burden of it upon them; yea, and to be very thankful to them too, that they will be at the pains, and can have the patience, to govern and live publicly. Therefore it is happy for the world that there are some who are born and bred up to it; and that custom hath made it easy, or at least tolerable to them. . . . The advantage which men have by a more devout and retired and contemplative life, is, that they are not distracted about many things; their minds and affections are set upon one thing; and the whole stream and force of their affections run one way. All their thoughts and endeavours are united in one great end and design, which makes their life all of a piece, and to be consistent with itself throughout.'

63

WHEN I started this book I warned the reader that perhaps the only thing of which I was certain was that I was certain of nothing else. I was trying to put my thoughts on sundry subjects in order and I asked no one to agree with me in my opinions. On revising what I have written, I have cut out the words, I think, in a great many places because, though they came to my pen naturally, I found them tedious, but they are to be understood as qualifying my every statement. And now that I come to this last section of my book, I am constrained more anxiously than ever to repeat that what I give are my own private convictions. It may be that they are superficial. It may be that some of them are contradictory. It is unlikely that surmises that are the outcome of thoughts, feelings, and desires built up out of all sorts of haphazard experiences and coloured by a particular personality should fit with the logical precision of a proposition of Euclid. When I wrote of the drama and of fiction I wrote of what by practice I had some cognizance of, but now that I come to deal with matters of which philosophers treat I have no more special knowledge than can be acquired by any man who has lived for many years a busy and varied life. Life also is a school of philosophy, but it is like one of those modern kindergartens in which children are left to their own devices and work only at the subjects that arouse their interest. Their attention is drawn to what seems to have a meaning for them and they take no notice of what does not immediately concern them. In psychological laboratories rats are trained to find their way through a maze and presently by trial and error they learn the path that leads to the food they seek. In the matters with which I now occupy myself I am like one of these rats scurrying along the pathways of the complicated maze, but I do not know that it has a centre where I shall find what I seek. For all I know all the alleys are blind.

I was introduced to philosophy by Kuno Fischer whose lectures I attended when I was at Heidelberg. He had a great reputation there and he was giving that winter a course of lectures on Schopenhauer. They were crowded and one had to queue up early in order to get a good seat. He was a dapper, short, stoutish man, neat in his dress, with a bullet head, white hair *en brosse* and a red face. His little eyes were quick and shining. He had a funny, flattened snub nose that looked as if it had been bashed in, and you would have been much more likely to take him for an old prize-fighter than for a philosopher. He was a humorist; he had indeed written a book on wit which I read at the time, but which I have completely forgotten, and every now and then a great guffaw broke from his audience of students as he made a joke. His voice was powerful and he was a vivid, impressive and exciting speaker. I was too young and too ignorant to understand much of what he said, but I got a very clear impression of Schopenhauer's odd and original personality and a confused feeling of the dramatic value and the romantic quality of his system. I hesitate to make any statement after so many years, but I have a notion that Kuno Fischer treated it as a work of art rather than as a serious contribution to metaphysics.

Since then I have read a great deal of philosophy. I have found it very good reading. Indeed, of the various great subjects that afford reading matter to the person for whom reading is a need and a delight it is the most varied, the most copious and the most satisfying. Ancient Greece is thrilling, but from this point of view there is not enough in it; a time comes when you have read the little that remains of its literature and all of significance that has been written about it. The Italian Renaissance is fascinating too, but the subject, comparatively, is small; the ideas that informed it were few, and you get tired of its art which has been long since drained of its creative value so that you are left only with grace, charm and symmetry (qualities of which you can have enough) and you get tired of its men, whose versatility falls into too uniform a pattern. You can go on reading about the Italian Renaissance for ever, but your interest fails before the material is exhausted. The French Revolution is another subject that may well engage the attention and it has the advantage that its significance is actual. It is close to us in point of time so that with a very small effort of imagination we can put ourselves into the men who made it. They are almost contemporaries. And what they did and what they thought affect the lives we lead to-day; after a fashion we are all descendants of the French Revolution. And the material is abundant. The documents that relate to it are countless and the last thing has never been said about it. You can always find something fresh and interesting to read. But it does not satisfy. The art and literature it directly produced are negligible, so that you are driven to the study of the men who made it, and the more you read about them the more are you dismayed by their pettiness and vulgarity. The actors in one of the greatest dramas in the world's history were pitifully inadequate to their parts. You turn away from the subject at last with a faint disgust.

But metaphysics never lets you down. You can never come to the end of it. It is as various as the soul of man. It has greatness, for it deals with nothing less than the whole of knowledge. It treats of the universe, of God and immortality, of the properties of human reason and the end and purpose of life, of the power and limitations of man; and if it cannot answer the questions that assail him on his journey through this dark and mysterious world it persuades him to support his ignorance with good humour. It teaches resignation and inculcates courage. It appeals to the imagination as well as to the intelligence; and to the amateur, much more, I suppose, than to the professional, it affords matter for that reverie which is the most delicious pleasure with which man can beguile his idleness.

Since, inspired by Kuno Fischer's lectures, I began to read Schopenhauer I have read pretty well all the most important works of the great classical philosophers. Though there is in them a great deal that I did not understand, and perhaps I did not even understand as much as I thought, I have read them with passionate interest. The only one who has consistently bored me is Hegel. This is doubtless my own fault, for his influence on philosophical thought during the nineteenth century proves his importance. I found him terribly long-winded and I could never reconcile myself to the jugglery with which it seemed to me he proved whatever he had a mind to. Perhaps I was prejudiced against him by the scorn with which Schopenhauer always spoke of him. But to the others, from Plato onwards, I surrendered myself, one after the other, with the pleasure of a traveller adventuring into an unknown country. I did not read critically, but as I might have read a novel, for the excitement and delight of it. (I have already confessed that I read a novel not for instruction, but for pleasure. I crave my reader's indulgence.) A student of character, I got an immense amount of pleasure out of the self-revelation which these various writers offered to my survey. I saw the man behind his philosophy and I was exalted by the nobility I found in some and amused by the queerness I discerned in others. I felt a wonderful exhilaration when I dizzily followed Plotinus in his flight from the alone to the alone, and though I have learnt since that Descartes drew preposterous conclusions from his effective premiss I was entranced by the lucidity of his expression. To read him was like swimming in a lake so clear that you could see the bottom; that crystalline water was wonderfully refreshing. I look upon my first reading of Spinoza as one of the signal experiences of my life. It filled me with just that feeling of majesty and exulting power that one has at the sight of a great mountain range.

And when I came to the English philosophers, with perhaps a slight prejudice, for it had been impressed upon me in Germany that, with the possible exception of Hume, they were quite negligible and Hume's only importance was that Kant had demolished him, I found that besides being philosophers they were uncommonly good writers. And though they might not be very great thinkers, of this I could not presume to judge, they were certainly very curious men. I should think that few could read Hobbes' Leviathan without being taken by the gruff, downright John Bullishness of his personality and surely no one could read Berkeley's Dialogues without being ravished by the charm of that delightful bishop. And though it may be true that Kant made hay of Hume's theories it would be impossible, I think, to write philosophy with more elegance, urbanity and clearness. They all, and Locke too for the matter of that, wrote English that the student of style could do much worse than study. Before I start writing a novel I read Candide over again so that I may have in the back of my mind the touchstone of that lucidity, grace and wit; I have a notion that it would not hurt the English philosophers of our own day if before they set about a work they submitted themselves to the discipline of reading Hume's Inquiry Concerning the Human Understanding. For it is not invariably that they write now with distinction. It may be that their thoughts are so much more subtle than those of their predecessors that they are obliged to use a technical vocabulary of their own invention; but it is a dangerous procedure, and when they deal with matters that are of pressing concern to all reflective persons, one can only regret that they cannot make their meaning so plain that all who read may understand. They tell me that Professor Whitehead has the most ingenious brain of anyone who is now engaged in philosophic thought. It seems to me a pity then that he should not always take pains to make his sense clear. It was a good rule of Spinoza's to indicate the nature of things by words whose customary meanings should not be altogether opposed to the meanings he desired to bestow upon them.

64

THERE IS no reason why philosophers should not be also men of letters. But to write well does not come by instinct; it is an art that demands arduous study. The philosopher does not speak only to other philosophers and to undergraduates working for a degree; he speaks also to the men of letters, politicians and reflective persons who directly mould the ideas of the coming generation. They, naturally enough, are taken by a philosophy that is striking and not too difficultly assimilated. We all know how the philosophy of Nietzsche has affected some parts of the world and few would assert that its influence has been other than disastrous. It has prevailed, not by such profundity of thought as it may have, but by a vivid style and an effective form. The philosopher who will not take the trouble to make himself clear shows only that he thinks his thought of no more than academic value.

It has, however, been a consolation to me to discover that sometimes even the professional philosophers do not understand one another. Bradley frequently confesses that he is at a loss to understand what someone with whom he is arguing means and Professor Whitehead in one place states that something Bradley says is beyond his comprehension. When the most eminent philosophers cannot always understand one another the layman may well feel resigned if he often does not understand them. Of course metaphysics is difficult. One must expect that. The layman walks a tight-rope without a pole to balance him and he must be thankful if he can scramble somehow to safety. The feat is exciting enough to make it worth his while to risk a tumble.

I was much disconcerted by the claim that I found here and there advanced that philosophy was the province of the higher mathematicians; and though it seemed hard to me to believe that, if knowledge, as the doctrine of evolution suggests, has been developed for practical reasons in the struggle for existence, the sum total of it, something that is essential to the well-being of man in general, could be reserved only for a small body of men who are gifted by nature with a rare faculty, I might very well have been deterred from pursuing my pleasant studies in this direction, since I have no head for mathematics, if I had not luckily come across an admission of Bradley's that he knew very little of this abstruse science. And Bradley was no mean philosopher. We know that the sense of taste differs in various persons; but without it men would perish. It seems as unlikely that you may not hold reasonable theories about the universe and man's place in it, the mystery of evil and the meaning of reality, unless you are a mathematical physicist, as that you cannot enjoy a bottle of wine unless you have the trained sensibility that enables you without error to ascribe a year to twenty different clarets.

For philosophy is not a subject that has to do only with philosophers and mathematicians. It is one that concerns us all. It is true that most of us accept our opinions on the matters with which it deals at second hand and most do not know that they have any philosophy at all. But it is implicit even in the most thoughtless. The old woman who first said, 'it's no good crying over spilt milk' was a philosopher in her way. For what did she mean by this except that regret was useless? A complete system of philosophy is implied. The determinist thinks that you cannot take a step in life that is not motivated by what you are at the moment; and you are not only your muscles, your nerves, your entrails and your brain; you are your habits, your opinions and your ideas. However little you may be aware of them, however contradictory, unreasonable and prejudiced they may be, they are there, influencing your actions and reactions. Even if you have never put them into words they are your philosophy. Perhaps it is well enough that most people should leave this unformulated. It is hardly thoughts they have, at least not conscious thoughts, it is a kind of vague feeling, a sort of experience like that muscular sense that the physiologists not so long ago discovered, which they have absorbed from the notions current in the society in which they live and which has been faintly modified by their own experience. They lead their ordered lives and this confused body of ideas and feelings is enough. Since it includes something of the wisdom of the ages, it is adequate for the ordinary purposes of the ordinary life. But I have sought to make a pattern of mine and from an early age tried to find out what were the elements I had to deal with. I wanted to get what knowledge I could about the general structure of the universe; I wanted to make up my mind whether I had to consider only this life or a life to come; I wanted to discover whether I was a free agent or whether my feeling that I could mould myself according to my will was an illusion; I wanted to know whether life had any meaning or whether it was I that must strive to give it one. So in a desultory way I began to read.

65

THE FIRST subject that attracted my attention was religion. For it seemed to me of the greatest importance to decide whether this world I lived in was the only one I had to reckon with or whether I must look upon it as no more than a place of trial which was to prepare me for a life to come. When I wrote Of Human Bondage I gave a chapter to my hero's loss of the faith in which he had been brought up. The book was read in typescript by a very clever woman who at that time was good enough to be interested in me. She told me that this chapter was inadequate. I rewrote it; but I do not think I much improved it. For it described my own experience and I have no doubt that my reasons for coming to the conclusion I came to were inadequate. They were the reasons of an ignorant boy. They were of the heart rather than of the head. When my parents died I went to live with my uncle who was a clergyman. He was a childless man of fifty, and I am sure that it was a great nuisance to have the charge of a small boy thrust upon him. He read prayers morning and evening, and we went to church twice on Sundays. Sunday was the busy day. My uncle always said that he was the only man in his parish who worked seven days a week. In point of fact he was incredibly idle and left the work of his parish to his curate and his churchwardens. But I was impressionable and soon became very religious. I accepted what I was taught, both in my uncle's vicarage and afterwards at school, with unquestioning trust.

There was one point that immediately affected me. I had not been long at school before I discovered, through the ridicule to which I was exposed and the humiliations I suffered, how great a misfortune it was to me that I stammered; and I had read in the Bible that if you had faith you could move mountains. My uncle assured me that it was a literal fact. One night, when I was going back to school next day, I prayed to God with all my might that he would take away my impediment; and, such was my faith, I went to sleep quite certain that when I awoke next morning I should be able to speak like everybody else. I pictured to myself the surprise of the boys (I was still at a preparatory school) when they found that I no longer stammered. I woke full of exultation and it was a real, a terrible shock, when I discovered that I stammered as badly as ever.

I grew older. I went to the King's School. The masters were clergymen; they were stupid and irascible. They were impatient of my stammering and if they did not ignore me completely, which I preferred, they bullied me. They seemed to think it was my fault that I stammered. Presently I discovered that my uncle was a selfish man who cared for nothing but his own comfort. The neighbouring clergy sometimes came to the vicarage. One of them was fined in the county court for starving his cows; another had to resign his living because he was convicted of drunkenness. I was taught that we lived in the presence of God and that the chief business of man was to save his soul. I could not help seeing that none of these clergymen practised what they preached. Fervent though my faith was, I had been terribly bored by all the church-going that was forced upon me, both at home and at school, and on going to Germany I welcomed the freedom that enabled me to stay away. But two or three times out of curiosity I went to High Mass at the Jesuit Church in Heidelberg. Though my uncle had a natural sympathy for Catholics (he was a High Churchman and at election time they painted on the garden fence, 'This way to Rome'), he had no doubt that they would frizzle in hell. He believed implicitly in eternal punishment. He hated the dissenters in his parish and indeed thought it a monstrous thing that the state tolerated them. His consolation was that they too would suffer eternal damnation. Heaven was reserved for the members of the Church of England. I accepted it as a great mercy of God that I had been bred in that communion. It was as wonderful as being born an Englishman.

But when I went to Germany I discovered that the Germans were just as proud of being Germans as I was proud of being English. I heard them say that the English did not understand music and that Shakespeare was only appreciated in Germany. They spoke of the English as a nation of shop-keepers and had no doubt in their minds that as artists, men of science and philosophers they were greatly superior. It shook me. And now at High Mass in Heidelberg I could not but notice that the students, who filled the church to its doors, seemed very devout. They had, indeed, all the appearance of believing in their religion as sincerely as I believed in mine. It was queer that they could, for of course I knew that theirs was false and mine was true. I think I can have had by nature no strong religious feeling, or else in the intolerance of my youth I must have been so shocked by the contrast of the practice with the professions of the various clergymen with whom I had to do, that I was already inclined to doubt; otherwise I can hardly think that such a simple little notion as then occurred to me could have had consequences that were to me of so much importance. It struck me that I might very well have been born in South Germany, and then I should naturally have been brought up as a Catholic. I found it very hard that thus through no fault of my own I should have been condemned to everlasting torment. My ingenuous nature revolted at the injustice. The next step was easy; I came to the conclusion that it could not matter a row of pins what one believed; God could not condemn people just because they were Spaniards or Hottentots. I might have stopped there and if I had been less ignorant adopted some form of deism like that which was current in the eighteenth century. But the beliefs that had been instilled into me hung together and when one of them came to seem outrageous the others participated in its fate. The whole horrible structure, based not on the love of God but on the fear of Hell, tumbled down like a house of cards.

With my mind at all events I ceased to believe in God; I felt the exhilaration of a new freedom. But we do not believe only with our minds; in some deep recess of my soul there lingered still the old dread of hell-fire, and for long my exultation was tempered by the shadow of that ancestral anxiety. I no longer believed in God; I still, in my bones, believed in the Devil.

66

IT WAS this fear that I sought to banish when, becoming a medical student, I entered a new world. I read a great many books. They told me that man was a machine subject to mechanical laws; and when the machine ran down that was the end of him. I saw men die at the hospital and my startled sensibilities confirmed what my books had taught me. I was satisfied to believe that religion and the idea of God were constructions that the human race had evolved as a convenience for living, and represented something that had at one time, and for all I was prepared to say still had, value for the survival of the species, but that must be historically explained and corresponded to nothing real. I called myself an agnostic, but in my blood and my bones I looked upon God as a hypothesis that a reasonable man must reject.

But if there was no God who could consign me to eternal flames and no soul that could be thus consigned, if I was the plaything of mechanical forces and the struggle for life was the impelling force, I could not see that there was any meaning in good such as I had been taught it. I began to read Ethics. I waded conscientiously through many formidable tomes. I came to the conclusion that man aimed at nothing but his own pleasure and that when he sacrificed himself for others it was only an illusion that led him to believe that he was seeking anything but his own gratification. And since the future was uncertain it was only common sense to seize every pleasure that the moment offered. I decided that right and wrong were merely words and that the rules of conduct were no more than conventions that men had set up to serve their own selfish purposes. The free man had no reason to follow them except in so far as they suited his convenience. Having then an epigrammatic turn, and epigrams being the fashion, I put my conviction into a phrase and said to myself: follow your inclinations with due regard to the policeman round the corner. By the time I was twenty-four I had constructed a complete system of philosophy. It rested on two principles: The Relativity of Things and The Circumferentiality of Man. I have learnt since that the first of these was not a very original discovery. It may be that the other was profound, but though I have racked my brains I cannot for the life of me remember what on earth it meant.

On a certain occasion I read a little story that greatly took my fancy. It is to be found in one of the volumes of Anatole France's La Vie Littéraire. It is many years since I read it, but it has remained in my recollection as follows: a young king of the East, anxious on his ascent of the throne to rule his kingdom justly, sent for the wise men of his country and ordered them to gather the wisdom of the world in books so that he might read them and learn how best to conduct himself. They went away and after thirty years returned with a string of camels laden with five thousand tomes. Here, they told him, is collected everything that wise men have learnt of the history and destiny of man. But the king was immersed in affairs of state and could not read so many books, so he bade them go and condense this knowledge into a smaller number. Fifteen years later they returned and their camels carried but five hundred works. In these volumes, they told the king, you will find all the wisdom of the world. But there were still too many and the king sent them away again. Ten years passed and they came back and now they brought no more than fifty books. But the king was old and tired. He had no time now even to read so few and he ordered his wise men once more to reduce their number and in a single volume give him an epitome of human knowledge so that he might learn at last what it was so important for him to know. They went away and set to work and in five years returned. They were old men when for the last time they came and laid the result of their labours in the king's hands, but now the king was dying and he had no time any more to read even the one book they brought him.

It was some such book as this that I sought, a book that would answer once for all the questions that puzzled me, so that, everything being settled for good and all, I could pursue the pattern of my life without let or hindrance. I read and read. From the classical philosophers I turned to the moderns, thinking that among them, perhaps, I should find what I wanted. I could not discover much agreement among them. I found myself convinced by the critical parts of their works, but when I came to the constructive, though often I failed to see the flaws, I could not but be conscious that they did not compel my assent. The impression suggested itself to me that notwithstanding their learning, their logic and their classifications, philosophers embraced such and such beliefs not because they were led to them by their reason, but because their temperaments forced these beliefs upon them. Otherwise I could not understand how after all this time they differed from one another so profoundly. When I read, I do not know where, that Fichte had said that the kind of philosophy a man adopts depends on the kind of man he is, it occurred to me that perhaps I was looking for something that could not be found. It seemed to me then that if there was in philosophy no universal truth that everyone could accept, but only a truth that agreed with the personality of the individual, the only thing for me was to narrow my search and look for some philosopher whose system suited me because I was the same sort of man that he was. The answers that he would provide to the questions that puzzled me must satisfy me because they would be the only possible answers to fit my humour.

For some time I was much attracted by the pragmatists. I had not got as much profit as I expected from the metaphysical writings of the dons at the great English universities. They seemed to me too gentlemanlike to be very good philosophers and I could not resist the suspicion that sometimes they failed to pursue an argument to its logical conclusion for fear of offending the susceptibilities of colleagues with whom they were in social relations. The pragmatists had vigour. They were very much alive. The most important of them wrote well, and they gave an appearance of simplicity to problems which I had not been able to make head or tail of. But much as I should have liked to I could not bring myself to believe, as they did, that truth is fashioned by us to meet our practical needs. The sense-datum, on which I thought all knowledge was based, seemed to me something given, which had to be accepted whether it suited the convenience or not. Nor did I feel comfortable with the argument that God existed if it consoled me to believe that he did. The pragmatists ceased to interest me so much. I found Bergson good to read, but singularly unconvincing; nor did I find in Benedetto Croce anything to my purpose. On the other hand, in Bertrand Russell I discovered a writer who greatly pleased me; he was easy to understand and his English was good. I read him with admiration.

I was very willing to accept him as the guide I sought. He had worldly wisdom and common sense. He was tolerant of human weakness. But I discovered in time that he was a guide none too certain of the way. His mind was restless. He was like an architect who, when you want a house to live in, having persuaded you to build it of brick, then sets before you good reasons why it should be built of stone; but when you have agreed to this produces reasons just as good to prove that the only material to use is reinforced concrete. Meanwhile you have not a roof to your head. I was looking for a system of philosophy as coherent and self-contained as Bradley's, in which one part hung necessarily on another, so that nothing could be altered without the whole fabric falling to pieces. This Bertrand Russell could not give me.

At last I came to the conclusion that I could never find the one, complete and satisfying book I sought, because that book could only be an expression of myself. So with more courage than discretion I made up my mind that I must write it for myself. I found out what were the books set for the undergraduate to read in order to take a philosophical degree and laboriously perused them. I thought I should thus have at least a foundation for my own work. It seemed to me that with this, the knowledge of the world I had acquired during the forty years of my life (for I was forty when I conceived this idea) and the industrious study of philosophical literature to which I was prepared to devote some years, I should be competent to write such a book as I had in mind. I was aware that except to myself it could have no value beyond such a coherent portrait as it might give of the soul (for want of a more exact word) of a reflective person who had led a fuller life and been subject to more varied experiences than generally fall to the lot of professional philosophers. I knew very well that I had no gift for metaphysical speculation. I meant to take from here and there theories that satisfied not only my mind but, what I could not but think more important than my mind, the whole body of my instincts, feelings and deep-rooted prejudices, the prejudices that are so intimate a part of one that they can hardly be distinguished from instincts; and out of them make a system that would be valid for me and enable me to pursue the course of my life.

But the more I read the more complicated the subject seemed to me and the more conscious I grew of my ignorance. I was peculiarly discouraged by the philosophical magazines in which I found topics discussed at great length which were evidently of importance but which seemed to me in my darkness very trivial; and the manner in which they were handled, the logical apparatus, the care with which each point was argued and the possible objections met, the terms which each writer defined when he first used them, the authorities he quoted proved to me that philosophy, at all events now, was a business for the experts to deal with between them. The layman could little hope to comprehend its subtleties. I should need twenty years to prepare myself to write the book I proposed and by the time it was done I might, like the king in Anatole France's story, be on my death bed and to me at least the labour I had taken would no longer be of use.

I abandoned the idea and all I have to show for my efforts now is the few desultory notes that follow. I claim no originality for them, or even for the words in which I have put them. I am like a tramp who has rigged himself up as best he could with a pair of trousers from a charitable farmer's wife, a coat off a scarecrow, odd boots out of a dustbin, and a hat that he has found in the road. They are just shreds and patches, but he has fitted himself into them pretty comfortably and, uncomely as they may be, he finds that they suit him well enough. When he passes a gentleman in a smart blue suit, a new hat and well-polished shoes, he thinks he looks very grand, but he is not so sure that in that neat and respectable attire he would be nearly so much at his ease as in his own rags and tatters.

67

WHEN I read Kant I found myself obliged to abandon the materialism in which in my youth I had exulted and the physiological determinism that went with it. I did not then know the objections that have riddled Kant's system and I found an emotional satisfaction in his philosophy. It excited me to contemplate that unknowable 'thing in itself' and I was content with a world that man had constructed from appearances. It gave me a peculiar sense of liberation. I jibbed at his maxim that you should so act that your action may be a universal rule. I was too much convinced of the diversity of human nature to believe that this was reasonable. I thought that what was right for one person might very well be wrong for another. For my part I chiefly wanted to be let alone, but I had discovered that not many wanted that, and if I let them alone they thought me unkind, indifferent and selfish. But one cannot study the idealistic philosophers long without coming into touch with solipsism. Idealism is always trembling on the brink of it. The philosophers shy away from it like startled fawns, but their arguments continue to lead them back to it and so far as I can judge they escape it only because they will not pursue them to the end. It is a theory that can hardly fail to allure the writer of fiction. The claims it makes are his common practice. It has a completeness and an elegance that make it infinitely attractive. Since I cannot suppose that everyone who reads this book will know all about the various philosophical systems, the instructed reader will perhaps forgive me if I state briefly what solipsism is. The solipsist believes only in himself and his experience. He creates the world as the theatre of his activity, and the world he creates consists of himself and his thoughts and feelings; and beyond that nothing has being. Every thing knowable, every fact of experience, is an idea in his mind, and without his mind does not exist. There is no possibility and no necessity for him to postulate anything outside himself. For him dream and reality are one. Life is a dream in which he creates the objects that come before him, a coherent and consistent dream, and when he ceases to dream, the world, with its beauty, its pain and sorrow and unimaginable variety, ceases to be. It is a perfect theory; it has but one defect; it is unbelievable.

When I cherished the ambition of writing a book on these matters, thinking I must start at the beginning, I studied epistemology. I found none of the theories that I examined very convincing. It seemed to me that the plain man (that object of the philosopher's contempt, except when it happens that his views agree with the philosopher's, in which case quite a lot of value is attached to them) incompetent to judge of their value was perhaps entitled to choose that one which most satisfied his pre-possessions. If one is unwilling to suspend one's judgement it appears to me that there is a good deal of plausibility in the theory which holds that, beyond certain fundamental data which they call the given, and the existence of other minds, which they infer, men can be sure of nothing. All the rest of their knowledge is fiction, the construction of their minds, that they have devised for the convenience of living. Having to fit themselves, in the course of evolution, to a constantly changing environment, they have made a picture from fragments that they took here and there because they suited their purposes. This is the world of phenomena that they know. Reality is merely the hypothesis they have suggested as its occasion. It may be that they might have taken other fragments and combined them into another picture. This different world would have been as coherent and as true as the one we imagine we know.

It would be difficult to persuade an author that there was not a close interaction between the body and the mind. The experience of Flaubert when he suffered from the symptoms of arsenical poisoning while writing of Emma Bovary's suicide is but an extreme instance of what every novelist has undergone. Most writers have chills and fevers, aches and pains, nausea at times, when they are engaged in composition; and contrariwise they are aware to what morbid states of their body they owe many of their happiest inventions. Knowing that many of their deepest emotions, many of the reflections that seem to come straight from heaven, may be due to want of exercise or a sluggish liver, they can hardly fail to regard their spiritual experiences with a certain irony; which is all to the good, for thus they can manage and manipulate them. For my part, of the various theories of the relations between matter and spirit that are offered by the philosophers for the consideration of the plain man that which still seems to me most satisfactory is Spinoza's conception that substance thinking and substance extended are one and the same substance. But of course to-day it is more convenient to call it energy. Unless I misunderstand him Bertrand Russell has expressed in his modern fashion an idea not very dissimilar when he speaks of a neutral stuff which is the raw material of the mental and physical worlds. Trying to form for myself some sort of picture of this, I have seen spirit in the likeness of a river that forces its way through the jungle of matter; but river is jungle and jungle is river, for river and jungle are one. It does not seem impossible that the biologists will in the future succeed in creating life in their laboratories and then it may be that we shall know more of these matters.

68

BUT THE plain man's interest in philosophy is practical. He wants to know what is the value of life, how he should live and what sense he can ascribe to the universe. When philosophers stand back and refuse to give even tentative answers to these questions they shirk their responsibilities. Now, the most urgent problem that confronts the plain man is the problem of evil.

It is curious to notice that when they speak of evil, philosophers so often use toothache as their example. They point out with justice that you cannot feel my toothache. In their sheltered, easy lives it looks as though this were the only pain that had much afflicted them and one might almost conclude that with the improvement of American dentistry the whole problem could be conveniently shelved. I have sometimes thought that it would be a very good thing if before philosophers were granted the degrees that will enable them to impart their wisdom to the young, they had to spend a year in social service in the slums of a great city or earn their living by manual labour. If they had ever seen a child die of meningitis they would face some of the problems that concern them with other eyes.

If the subject were not of such pressing moment it would be difficult to read the chapter on evil in Appearance and Reality without ironic amusement. It is appallingly gentlemanlike. It leaves you with the impression that it is really rather bad form to attach any great importance to evil, and though its existence must be admitted it is unreasonable to make a fuss about it. In any case it is much exaggerated and it is evident that there is a lot of good in it. Bradley held that there was no pain on the whole. The Absolute is the richer for every discord and for all diversity which it embraces. Just as in a machine, he tells us, the resistance and pressure of the parts subserve an end beyond any of them, so at a much higher level it may be with the Absolute; and if this is possible it is indubitably real. Evil and error subserve a wider scheme and in this are realized. They play a part in a higher good and in this sense unknowingly are good. Evil in short is a deception of our senses and nothing more.

I have tried to find out what philosophers of other schools had to say on this question. This is not very much. It may be that there is not very much to be said about it, and philosophers quite naturally attach importance to subjects upon which they can discourse at length. And in the little they have said I can find less to satisfy me. It may be that the evils we endure educate us and so make us better; but observation does not allow us to think that this is a universal rule. It may be that courage and sympathy are excellent and that they could not come into existence without danger and suffering. It is hard to see how the Victoria Cross that rewards the soldier who has risked his life to save a blinded man is going to solace *him* for the loss of his sight. To give alms shows charity, and charity is a virtue, but does *that* good compensate for the evil of the cripple whose poverty has called it forth? Evils are there, omnipresent; pain and disease, the death of those we love, poverty, crime, sin, frustrated hope: the list is interminable. What explanations have the philosophers to offer? Some say that evil is logically necessary so that we may know good; some say that by the nature of the world there is an opposition between good and evil and that each is metaphysically necessary to the other. What explanations have the theologians to offer? Some say that God has placed evils here for our training; some say that he has sent them upon men to punish them for their sins. But *I* have seen a child die of meningitis. I have only found one explanation that appealed equally to my sensibility and to my imagination. This is the doctrine of the transmigration of souls. As everyone knows, it assumes that life does not begin at birth or end at death, but is a link in an indefinite series of lives each one of which is determined by the acts done in previous existences. Good deeds may exalt a man to the heights of heaven and evil deeds degrade him to the depths of hell. All lives come to an end, even the life of the gods, and happiness is to be sought in release from the round of births and repose in the changeless state called Nirvana. It would be less difficult to bear the evils of one's own life if one could think that they were but the necessary outcome of one's errors in a previous existence, and the effort to do better would be less difficult too when there was the hope that in another existence a greater happiness would reward one. But if one feels one's own woes in a more forcible way than those of others (I cannot feel your toothache, as the philosophers say) it is the woes of others that arouse one's indignation. It is possible to achieve resignation in regard to one's own, but only philosophers obsessed with the perfection of the Absolute can look upon those of others, which seem so often unmerited, with an equal mind. If Karma were true one could look upon them with pity, but with fortitude. Revulsion would be out of place and life would be robbed of the meaninglessness of pain which is pessimism's unanswered argument. I can only regret that I find the doctrine as impossible to believe as the solipsism of which I spoke just now.

69

BUT I have not done with evil yet. The problem presses when you come to consider whether God exists, and if he does, what nature must be ascribed to him. The time came when, like everybody else, I read the engaging works of the physicists. I was seized with awe at the contemplation of the immense distances that separated the stars and the vast stretches of time that light traversed in order to come from them to us. I was staggered by the unimaginable extent of the nebulæ. If I understood aright what I read, I must suppose that at the beginning the two forces of cosmical attraction and repulsion balanced so that the universe remained for untold ages in a state of perfect equilibrium. Then at some moment this was disturbed and the universe, toppling off its balance, gave rise to the universe the astronomers tell us of and the little earth we know. But what caused the original act of creation and what upset the balance of equilibrium? I seemed inevitably drawn to the conception of a creator, and what could create this vast, this stupendous universe but a being all-powerful? But the evil of the world then forces on us the conclusion that this being cannot be all-powerful and all-good. A God who is all-powerful may be justly blamed for the evil of the world and it seems absurd to consider him with admiration or accord him worship. But mind and heart revolt against the conception of a God who is not all-good. We are forced then to accept the supposition of a God who is not all-powerful: such a God contains within himself no explanation of his own existence or of that of the universe he creates.

It is singular when you read the documents on which the great religions of the world are founded, to note how much more succeeding ages have read into them than was there. Their teaching, their example, have created an ideal greater than themselves. Most of us find it embarrassing when flowering compliments are paid to us. It is strange that the devout should think God can be pleased when they slavishly pay them to him. When I was young I had an elderly friend who used often to ask me to stay with him in the country. He was a religious man and he read prayers to the assembled household every morning. But he had crossed out in pencil all the passages in the Book of Common Prayer that praised God. He said that there was nothing so vulgar as to praise people to their faces and, himself a gentleman, he could not believe that God was so ungentlemanly as to like it. At the time it seemed to me a curious eccentricity. I think now that my friend showed very good sense.

Men are passionate, men are weak, men are stupid, men are pitiful; to bring to bear on them anything so tremendous as the wrath of God seems strangely inept. It is not very difficult to forgive other people their sins. When you put yourself into their shoes it is generally easy to see what has caused them to do things they should not have done and excuses can be found for them. There is a natural instinct of anger when some harm is done

one that leads one to revengeful action, and it is hard in what concerns oneself to take up an attitude of detachment; but a little reflection enables one to look upon the situation from the outside and with practice it is no more difficult to forgive the harm that is done one than any other. It is much harder to forgive people the harm one has done them; that indeed requires a singular power of mind.

Every artist wishes to be believed in, but he is not angry with those who will not accept the communication he offers. God is not so reasonable. He craves so urgently to be believed in that you might think he needed your belief in order to reassure himself of his own existence. He promises rewards to those who believe in him and threatens with horrible punishment those who do not. For my part I cannot believe in a God who is angry with me because I do not believe in him. I cannot believe in a God who is less tolerant than I. I cannot believe in a God who has neither humour nor common sense. Plutarch long ago put the matter succinctly. 'I would much rather,' he writes, 'have men say of me that there never was a Plutarch, nor is now, than to say that Plutarch is a man inconstant, fickle, easily moved to anger, revengeful for trifling provocations and vexed at small things.'

But though men have ascribed to God imperfections that they would deplore in themselves that does not prove that God does not exist. It proves only that the religions that men have accepted are but blind alleys cut into an impenetrable jungle and none of them leads to the heart of the great mystery. Arguments have been adduced to prove the existence of God, and I will ask the reader to have patience with me while I briefly consider them. One of them assumes that man has an idea of a perfect being; and since perfection includes existence a perfect being must exist. Another maintains that every event has a cause and since the universe exists it must have a cause and this cause is the Creator. A third, the argument from design, which Kant said was the clearest, oldest and best suited to human reason, is thus stated by one of the characters in Hume's great dialogues: 'the order and arrangement of nature, the curious adjustment of final causes, the plain use and intention of every part and organ; all these bespeak in the clearest language an intelligent cause or Author.' But Kant showed conclusively that there was no more to be said in favour of this argument than in that of the other two. In their place he propounded another. In a few words it is to the effect that without God there is no guarantee that the sense of duty, which presupposes a free and real self, is not an illusion and therefore that it is morally necessary to believe in God. This has been generally thought more creditable to Kant's amiable nature than to his subtle intelligence. The argument which to me seems more persuasive than any of these is one that has now fallen out of favour. It is known as the proof *e consensu gentium*. It asserts that all men from the remotest origins have had some sort of belief in God and it is hard to think that a belief that has grown up with the human race, a belief that has been accepted by the wisest men, the sages of the East, the philosophers of Greece, the great Scholastics, should not have a foundation in fact. It has seemed to many instinctive and it may be (one can only say, it may be, for it is far from certain) that an instinct does not exist unless there is a possibility of its being satisfied. Experience has shown that the prevalence of a belief, no matter for how long it has been held, is no guarantee of its truth. It appears, then, that none of the arguments for the existence of God is valid. But of course you do not disprove his existence because you cannot prove it. Awe remains, man's sense of helplessness, and his desire to attain harmony between himself and the universe at large. These, rather than the worship of nature or of ancestors, magic or morality, are the sources of religion. There is no reason to believe that what you desire exists, but it is a hard saying that you have no right to believe what you cannot prove; there is no reason why you should not believe so long as you are aware that your belief lacks proof. I suppose that if your nature is such that you want comfort in your trials and a love that sustains and encourages you, you will neither ask for proofs nor have need of them. Your intuition suffices.

Mysticism is beyond proof and indeed demands no more than an indwelling conviction. It is independent of the creeds, for it finds sustenance in all of them, and it is so personal that it satisfies every idiosyncrasy. It is the feeling that the world we live in is but part of a spiritual universe and from this gains its significance; it is the sense of a present God who supports and comforts us. The mystics have narrated their experience so often, and in terms so similar, that I do not see how one can deny its reality. Indeed, I have myself had on one occasion an experience that I could only describe in the words the mystics have used to describe their ecstasy. I was sitting in one of the deserted mosques near Cairo when suddenly I felt myself rapt as Ignatius of Loyola was rapt when he sat by the river at Manresa. I had an overwhelming sense of the power and import of the universe, and an intimate, a shattering sense of communion with it. I could almost bring myself to say that I felt the presence of God. It is doubtless a common enough sensation and the mystics have been careful to ascribe value to it only if its influence was clearly seen in its results. I have a notion that it can be occasioned by other causes than the religious. The saints themselves have been willing to admit that the artists may have it, and love, as we know, can produce a state so like it that the mystics have found themselves drawn to use the phrases of lovers to express the beatific vision. I do not know that it is more mysterious than that condition, which the psychologists have not yet explained, when you have a strong feeling that you have at some past time been through an experience that you are in the act of undergoing. The ecstasy of the mystic is real enough, but it is valid only for himself. Mystic and sceptic agree in this, that at the end of all our intellectual efforts there remains a great mystery.

Faced with this, awed by the greatness of the universe and malcontent with what the philosophers told me, and what the saints, I have sometimes gone back,

185

beyond Mohammed, Jesus and Buddha, beyond the gods of Greece, Jehovah and Baal, to the Brahma of the Upanisads. That spirit, if spirit it may be called, self-created and independent of all other existence, though all that exists, exists in it, the sole source of life in all that lives, has at least a grandeur that satisfies the imagination. But I have been busy with words too long not to be suspicious of them, and when I look at those I have just written, I cannot but see that their meaning is tenuous. In religion above all things the only thing of use is an objective truth. The only God that is of use is a being who is personal, supreme and good, and whose existence is as certain as that two and two make four. I cannot penetrate the mystery. I remain an agnostic, and the practical outcome of agnosticism is that you act as though God did not exist.

70

BELIEF IN God is not essential to belief in immortality, but it is difficult to dissociate one from the other. Even in that shadowy form of survival which looks forward to the dissolution of human consciousness, once divorced from the body, into the general consciousness, it is only possible to refuse the name of God to this general consciousness if you deny that it has either efficacy or value. And practically, as we know, the two notions have been so inseparably connected that a life after death has always been looked upon as the most powerful instrument to God's hand in his dealings with the human race. It has offered a merciful God the happiness of rewarding the good and a revengeful one the satisfaction of punishing the wicked. The arguments for immortality are simple enough, but, if not meaningless, they have no great force unless the premiss of God's existence is accepted first. I will nevertheless enumerate them. One is based on the incompleteness of life: we have a craving to fulfil ourselves, but the force of events, and our own limitations, leave us with a sense of frustration and this a future life will counterbalance. So Goethe, though he did so much, felt that there was still more for him to do. Akin to this is the argument from desire: if we can conceive immortality and if we desire it, does not that indicate that it exists? Our immortal longings can be understood only by the possibility of their satisfaction. Another argument insists upon the indignation, the anguish and perplexity that beset men when they consider the injustice and the inequality that reign in this world. The wicked flourish like the green bay-tree. Justice demands another life in which the guilty may be punished and the innocent rewarded. Evil can be condoned only if in the beyond it is compensated by good and God himself needs immortality to vindicate his ways to man. Then there is the idealistic argument: consciousness cannot be extinguished by death; for the annihilation of consciousness is inconceivable, since only consciousness can conceive the annihilation of consciousness; it goes on to assert that values exist only for mind and point to a supreme mind in which they are completely realized. If God is love, men are values to him, and it cannot be believed that what is of value to God can be allowed to perish. But at this point a certain hesitation has betrayed itself. Common experience, especially the common experience of philosophers, shows that a great many men are no great shakes. Immortality is too stupendous a notion to be entertained in connection with common mortals. They are too insignificant to deserve eternal punishment or to merit eternal bliss. So philosophers have been found to suggest that such as have the possibility of spiritual fulfilment will enjoy a limited survival till they have had the opportunity of reaching the perfection of which they are capable and will then suffer a welcome extinction, while those who have no such possibility will be forthwith mercifully annihilated. But when one comes to enquire into the qualities which in this case will admit the chosen few into the blessings of this limited survival one makes the disconcerting discovery that they are those that few but philosophers possess. One cannot but wonder, however, in what manner the philosophers will pass their time when their virtue has received its due reward, for the questions that occupied them during their sojourn on earth will presumably have received their adequate replies. One can only suppose that they will take piano lessons from Beethoven or learn to paint in water colour under the guidance of Michelangelo. Unless these two great men have much changed they will find them irascible masters.

A very good test of the force of arguments on which you accept a belief is to ask yourself whether for reasons of equal weight you would embark on a practical operation of any importance. Would you for example buy a house on hearsay without having the title examined by a lawyer and the drains tested by a surveyor? The arguments for immortality, weak when you take them one by one, are no more cogent when you take them together. They are alluring, like a house-agent's advertisement in the daily paper, but to me at least no more convincing. For my part I cannot see how consciousness can persist when its physical basis has been destroyed and I am too sure of the interconnection of my body and my mind to think that any survival of my consciousness apart from my body would be in any sense the survival of myself. Even if one could persuade oneself that there was any truth in the suggestion that the human consciousness survives in some general consciousness, there would be small comfort in it, and to be satisfied with the notion that one survives in such spiritual force as one has produced is merely to cheat oneself with idle words. The only survival that has any value is the complete survival of the individual.

71

IF THEN one puts aside the existence of God and the possibility of survival as too doubtful to have any effect on one's behaviour, one has to make up one's mind what is the meaning and use of life. If death ends all, if I have neither to hope for good to come nor to fear evil, I must ask myself what I am here for and how in these circumstances I must conduct myself. Now the answer to one of these questions is plain, but it is so unpalatable that most men will not face it. There is no reason for life and life has no meaning. We are here, inhabitants for a little while of a small planet, revolving round a minor star which in its turn is a member of one of unnumbered galaxies. It may be that this planet alone can support life, or it may be that in other parts of the universe other planets have had the possibility of forming a suitable environment to that substance from which, we suppose, along the vast course of time the men we are have been gradually created. And if the astronomer tells us truth this planet will eventually reach a condition when living things can no longer exist upon it and at long last the universe will attain that final stage of equilibrium when nothing more can happen. Æons and æons before this man will have disappeared. Is it possible to suppose that it will matter then that he ever existed? He will have been a chapter in the history of the universe as pointless as the chapter in which is written the life stories of the strange monsters that inhabited the primæval earth.

I must ask myself then what difference all this makes to me and how I am to deal with these circumstances if I want to make the best use of my life and to get the utmost that I can out of it. Here it is not I that speak, it is the craving within me, which is in every man, to persevere in my own being; it is the egoism that we all inherit from that remote energy which in the unplumbed past first set the ball rolling; it is the need of self-assertion which is in every living thing and which keeps it alive. It is the very essence of man. Its satisfaction is the self-satisfaction which Spinoza has told us is the highest thing for which we can hope, 'for no one endeavours to preserve his being for the sake of any end.' We may suppose that consciousness was kindled in man as an instrument to enable him to deal with his environment and that for long ages it reached no higher development than was needed to deal with the vital problems of his practice. But it seems in course of time to have outgrown his immediate needs, and with the rise of imagination man widened his environment to include the unseen. We know with what answers he satisfied the questions that he put to himself then. The energy that flamed within him was so intense that he could admit no doubt of his significance; his egoism was so all-embracing that he could not conceive the possibility of his extinction. To many these answers are satisfactory still. They give meaning to life and comfort to human vanity.

Most people think little. They accept their presence in the world; blind slaves of the striving which is their mainspring they are driven this way and that to satisfy their natural impulses, and when it dwindles they go out like the light of a candle. Their lives are purely instinctive. It may be that theirs is the greater wisdom. But if your consciousness has so far developed that you find certain questions pressing upon you and you think the old answers wrong, what are you going to do? What answers will you give? To at least one of these questions two of the wisest men who ever lived have given their own answers. When you come to look at them they seem to mean pretty much the same thing and I am not so sure that that is very much. Aristotle has said that the end of human activity is right action, and Goethe that the secret of life is living. I suppose that Goethe means that man makes the most of his life when he arrives at self-realization; he had small respect for a life governed by passing whims and uncontrolled instincts. But the difficulty of self-realization, that bringing to the highest perfection every faculty of which you are possessed, so that you get from life all the pleasure, beauty, emotion and interest you can wring from it, is that the claims of other people constantly limit your activity; and moralists, taken by the reasonableness of the theory, but frightened of its consequences, have spilt much ink to prove that in sacrifice and selflessness a man most completely realizes himself. That is certainly not what Goethe meant and it does not seem to be true. That there is a singular delight in self-sacrifice few would deny, and in so far as it offers a new field for activity and the opportunity to develop a new side of the self, it has value in self-realization; but if you aim at self-realization only in so far as it interferes with no one else's attempts at the same thing you will not get very far. Such an aim demands a good deal of ruthlessness and an absorption in oneself which is offensive to others and thus often stultifies itself. As we well know many of those who came in contact with Goethe were outraged by his frigid egotism.

72

IT MAY seem arrogant that I should not have been content to walk in the steps of men much wiser than myself. But much as we resemble one another we are none of us exactly alike (our finger-prints are there to show it), and I have seen no reason why I should not, so far as I could, choose my own course. I have sought to make a pattern of my life. This, I suppose, might be described as self-realization tempered by a lively sense of irony; making the best of a bad job. But a question presents itself which I shirked when, at the beginning of my book, I dealt with this subject; and now that I can avoid it no longer I cannot but draw back. I am conscious that here and there I have taken free-will for granted; I have spoken as though I had power to mould my intentions and direct my actions as the whim took me. In other places I have spoken as though I accepted determinism. Such shilly-shallying would have been deplorable had I been writing a philosophical work. I make no such pretension. But how can I, an amateur, be expected to settle a question which the philosophers have not yet ceased to argue?

It might seem only sensible to leave the matter alone, but it happens to be one in which the writer of fiction is peculiarly concerned. For as a writer he finds himself compelled by his readers to rigid determination. I pointed out earlier in these pages how unwilling an audience is to accept impulse on the stage. Now an impulse is merely an urge to action of whose motive the agent is not conscious; it is analogous to an intuition, which is a judgement you make without being aware of its grounds. But though an impulse has its motive, an audience, because it is not obvious, will not accept it. The spectators of a play and the readers of a book insist on knowing the reasons of action and they will not admit its probability unless the reasons are cogent. Each person must behave in character; that means that he must do what from their knowledge of him they expect him to do. Cunning must be exercised in order to persuade them to accept the coincidences and accidents which in real life they swallow without a second thought. They are determinists to a man and the writer who trifles with their obstinate prejudice is lost.

But when I look back upon my own life I cannot but notice how much that vitally affected me has been due to circumstances that it is hard not to regard as pure chance. Determinism tells us that choice follows the line of least resistance or the strongest motive. I am not conscious that I have always followed the line of least resistance, and if I have followed the strongest motive that motive has been an idea of myself that I have gradually evolved. The metaphor of chess, though frayed and shop-worn, is here wonderfully apposite. The pieces were provided and I had to accept the mode of action that was characteristic of each one; I had to accept the moves of the persons I played with; but it has seemed to me that I had the power to make on my side, in accordance perhaps with my likes and dislikes and the ideal that I set before me, moves that I freely willed. It has seemed to me that I have now and then been able to put forth an effort that was not wholly determined. If it was an illusion it was an illusion that had its own efficacy. The moves I made, I know now, were often mistaken, but in one way and another they have tended to the end in view. I wish that I had not committed a great many errors, but I do not deplore them nor would I now have them undone.

I do not think it unreasonable to hold the opinion that everything in the universe combines to cause every one of our actions, and this naturally includes all our opinions and desires; but whether an action, once performed, was inevitable from all eternity can only be decided when you have made up your mind whether or no there are events, the events that Dr. Broad calls causal progenitors, which are not completely determined. Hume long ago showed that there was no intrinsic connection between cause and effect which could be perceived by the mind; and of late the Principle of Indeterminacy, by bringing to view certain events to which apparently no causes can be assigned, has cast a doubt on the universal efficacy of those laws upon which science has hitherto been based. It looks as if chance must once more be reckoned with. But if we are not certainly bound by the law of cause and effect, then perhaps it is not an illusion that our wills are free. The bishops and the deans have snatched at this new notion as though it were the devil's tail by which they hoped to drag the old devil himself back into existence. There has been great rejoicing, if not in the courts of heaven, at all events in the palaces of the episcopacy. Perhaps the Te Deum has been sung too soon. It is well to remember that the two most eminent scientists of our day regard Heisenberg's principle with scepticism. Planck has stated his belief that further research will sweep away the anomaly, and Einstein has described the philosophical ideas that have been based upon it as 'literature'; I am afraid that this is only his civil way of calling them nonsense. The physicists themselves tell us that physics is making such rapid progress that it is only possible to keep abreast of it by a close study of the periodical literature. It is surely rash to found a theory on principles suggested by a science that is so unstable. Schrödinger himself has stated that a final and comprehensive judgement on the matter is at present impossible. The plain man is justified in sitting on the fence, but perhaps he is prudent to keep his legs dangling on the side of determinism.

73

THE LIFE force is vigorous. The delight that accompanies it counterbalances all the pains and hardships that confront men. It makes life worth living, for it works from within and lights with its own bright flame each one's circumstances so that, however intolerable, they yet seem tolerable to him. Much pessimism is caused by ascribing to others the feelings you would feel if you were in their place. It is this (among much else) that makes novels so false. The novelist constructs a public world out of his own private world and gives to the characters of his fancy a sensitiveness, a power of reflection and an emotional capacity, which are peculiar to himself. Most people have little imagination and they do not suffer from circumstances that to the imaginative would be unbearable. The lack of privacy, to take an instance, in which the very poor live seems frightful to us who value it; but it does not seem so to the very poor. They hate to be alone; it gives them a sense of security to live in company. No one who has dwelt among them can fail to have noticed how little they envy the well-to-do. The fact is that they do not want many of the things that to others of us appear essential. It is fortunate for the well-to-do. For he is blind who will not see that in the lives of the proletariat in the great cities all is misery and confusion. It is hard to reconcile oneself to the fact that men should have no work to do, that work should be so dreary, that they should live, they, their wives and their children, on the edge of starvation, and in the end have nothing to look forward to but destitution. If only revolution can remedy this, then let revolution come and come quickly. When we see the cruelty with which men even now treat one another in countries that we have been in the habit of calling civilized, it would be rash to say that they are any better than they were, but for all that it does not seem fatuous to think that the world is on the whole a better place to live in than it was in the past that history sets before us, and that the lot of the great majority, bad as it is, is less dreadful than it was then; and one may reasonably hope that with the increase of knowledge, with the discarding of many cruel superstitions and outworn conventions, with a livelier sense of loving-kindness, many of the evils from which men suffer will be removed. But many evils must continue to exist. We are the playthings of nature. Earthquakes will continue to wreak havoc, droughts to ruin crops and unforeseen floods to destroy the prudent constructions of men. Human folly, alas, will continue to devastate the nations with war. Men will continue to be born who are not fitted for life and life will be a burden to them. So long as some are strong and some are weak, the weak will be driven to the wall. So long as men are cursed with the sense of possession, and that I presume is as long as they exist, they will wrest what they can from those who are powerless to hold it. So long as they have the instinct of self-assertion, they will exercise it at the expense of others' happiness. In short, so long as man is man he must be prepared to face all the woes that he can bear.

There is no explanation for evil. It must be looked upon as a necessary part of the order of the universe. To ignore it is childish; to bewail it senseless. Spinoza called pity womanish; the epithet has a harsh sound on the lips of that tender and austere spirit. I suppose he thought that it was but waste of emotion to feel strongly about what you could not alter.

I am not a pessimist. Indeed, it would be non-sensical of me to be so, for I have been one of the lucky ones. I have often wondered at my good fortune. I am well aware that many who were more deserving than I have not had the happy fate that has befallen me. An accident here, an accident there, might have changed everything and frustrated me as so many with talents equal to, or greater than, mine, with equal opportunities, have been frustrated. Should any of them chance to read these pages, I would ask them to believe that I do not arrogantly ascribe to my merits what has come to me, but to some concatenation of unlikely circumstances for which I can offer no exp'anation. With all my limitations, physical and mental, I have been glad to live. I would not live my life over again. There would be no point in that. Nor would I care to pass again through the anguish I have suffered. It is one of the faults of my nature that I have suffered more from the pains, than I have enjoyed the pleasures, of my life. But without my physical imper-fections, with a stronger body and a better brain, I would not mind entering upon the world afresh. The years that now stretch immediately in front of us look as if they would be interesting. The young enter upon life now with advantages that were denied to the young of my generation. They are hampered by fewer conventions and they have learnt how great is the value of youth. The world of my twenties was a middle-aged world and youth was something to be got through as quickly as possible so that maturity might be reached. The young things of the present day, at least in that middle-class to which I belong, seem to me better prepared. They are taught now many things that are useful to them, whereas we had to pick them up as best we could. The relation between the sexes is more normal. Young women have learnt now to be the companions of young men. One of the difficulties that my generation had to face, the generation that saw the emancipation of women, was this: women had ceased to be the housekeepers and mothers of an earlier age, who led a life apart from men, with their own interests and particular concerns, and were trying to participate in men's affairs without the capacity to do so; they demanded the consideration that had been their due when they were content to look upon themselves as men's inferiors and withal insisted on their right, their new-won right, to join in all the masculine activities in which they knew only enough to make a nuisance of themselves. They were no longer housewives and had not yet learnt to be good fellows. There is no more pleasant spectacle for an elderly gentleman than that of the young girl of the present day, so competent and so self-assured, who can run an office and play a hard game of tennis, who is intelligently concerned with public affairs and can appreciate the arts, and prepared to stand on her own feet, faces life with cool, shrewd and tolerant eyes.

Far be it from me to don the prophet's mantle, but I think it is clear that these young folk who are now taking the stage must look forward to economic changes that will transform civilisation. They will not know the easy, sheltered life which makes many who were at their prime before the war look upon those years as did the survivors of the French Revolution when they looked back on the Ancien Régime. They will not know the *douceur de vivre*. We live now on the eve of great revolutions. I cannot doubt that the proletariat, increasingly conscious of its rights, will eventually seize power in one country after the other, and I never cease to marvel that the governing classes of to-day, rather than continue a vain struggle against these overwhelming forces, do not use every effort to train the masses for their future tasks so that when they are dispossessed their fate may be less cruel than that which befell them in Russia. Years ago Disraeli told them what to do. For my part I must candidly say that I hope the present state of things will last my time. But we live in an era of rapid change and I may yet see the countries of the west given over to the rule of communism. A Russian exile of my acquaintance told me that when he lost his estates and his wealth, he was overcome with despair; but at the end of a fortnight he regained his serenity and never since gave a thought to what he had been deprived of. I do not think I have such an attachment to my various possessions as to regret their loss for long. If such a condition of things came to pass in my world I should make an attempt to adapt myself and then, if I found life intolerable, I think I should not lack the courage to quit a stage on which I could no longer play my part to my own satisfaction. I wonder why so many people turn with horror from the thought of suicide. To speak of it as cowardly is nonsense. I can only approve the man who makes an end of himself of his own will when life has nothing to offer him but pain and misfortune. Did not Pliny say that the power of dying when you please is the best thing that God has given to man amid all the sufferings of life? Putting aside those who regard suicide as sinful because it breaks a divine law, I think the reason of the indignation which it seems to arouse in so many is that the suicide flouts the life-force, and by setting at nought the strongest instinct of human beings casts a terrifying doubt on its power to preserve them.

With this book I shall have completed in sufficient outline the pattern I set myself to make. If I live I shall write other books, for my amusement and I hope for the amusement of my readers, but I do not think they will add anything essential to my design. The house is built. There will be additions, a terrace from which one has a pretty view, or an arbour in which to meditate in the heat of summer; but should death prevent me from producing them, the house, though the housebreakers may set to work on it the day after I am buried in an obituary notice, will have been built.

I look forward to old age without dismay. When Lawrence of Arabia was killed I read in an article contributed by a friend that it was his habit to ride his motor-bicycle at an excessive speed with the notion that an accident would end his life while he was still in full possession of his powers and so spare him the indignity of old age. If this is true it was a great weakness in that strange and somewhat theatrical character. It showed want of sense. For the complete life, the perfect pattern, includes old age as well as youth and maturity. The beauty of the morning and the radiance of noon are good, but it would be a very silly person who drew the curtains and turned on the light in order to shut out the tranquillity of the evening. Old age has its pleasures, which, though different, are not less than the pleasures of youth. The philosophers have always told us that we are the slaves of our passions, and is it so small a thing to be liberated from their sway? The fool's old age will be foolish, but so was his youth. The young man turns away from it with horror because he thinks that when he reaches it, he will still yearn for the things that give variety and gusto to his youth. He is mistaken. It is true that the old man will no longer be able to climb an Alp or tumble a pretty girl on a bed; it is true that he can no longer arouse the concupiscence of others. It is something to be free from the pangs of unrequited love and the torment of jealousy. It is something that envy, which so often poisons youth, should be assuaged by the extinction of desire. But these are negative compensations; old age has positive compensations also. Paradoxical as it may sound it has more time. When I was young I was amazed at Plutarch's statement that the elder Cato began at the age of eighty to learn Greek. I am amazed no longer. Old age is ready to undertake tasks that youth shirked because they would take too long. In old age the taste improves and it is possible to enjoy art and literature without the personal bias that in youth warps the judgement. It has the satisfaction of its own fulfilment. It is liberated from the trammels of human egoism; free at last, the soul delights in the passing moment, but does not bid it stay. It has completed the pattern. Goethe asked for survival after death so that he might realize those sides of himself which he felt that in his life he had not had time to develop. But did he not say that he who would accomplish anything must learn to limit himself? When you read his life you cannot but be struck by the way in which he wasted time in trivial pursuits. Perhaps if he had limited himself more carefully he would have developed everything that properly belonged to his special individuality and so found no need of a future life.

74

SPINOZA SAYS that a free man thinks of nothing less than of death. It is unnecessary to dwell upon it, but it is foolish, as so many do, to shrink from all consideration of it. It is well to make up one's mind about it. It is impossible to know till death is there facing one whether one will fear it. I have often tried to imagine what my feelings would be if a doctor told me I had a fatal disease and had no more than a little time to live. I have put them into the mouths of various characters of my invention, but I am aware that thus I dramatized them and I cannot tell whether they would be those I should actually feel. I do not think I have a very strong instinctive hold on life. I have had a good many serious illnesses, but have only once known myself to be within measurable distance of death; then I was so tired that I could not fear, I only wanted to be done with the struggle. Death is inevitable and it does not much matter how one meets it. I do not think one can be blamed if one hopes that one will not be aware of its imminence and be fortunate enough to undergo it without pain.

I have always lived so much in the future that now, though the future is so short, I cannot get out of the habit and my mind looks forward with a certain complacency to the completion within an indefinite number of years of the pattern that I have tried to make. There are moments when I have so palpitating an eagerness for death that I could fly to it as to the arms of a lover. It gives me the same passionate thrill as years ago was given me by life. I am drunk with the thought of it. It seems to me then to offer me the final and absolute freedom. Notwithstanding, I am willing enough to go on living so long as the doctors can keep me in tolerable health; I enjoy the spectacle of the world and it interests me to see what is going to happen. The consummation of many lives that have run their course parallel with my own gives me continual food for reflection and sometimes for the confirmation of theories that I formed long ago. I shall be sorry to part from my friends. I cannot be indifferent to the welfare of some whom I have guided and protected, but it is well that after depending on me so long they should enjoy their liberty whithersoever it leads them. Having held a certain place in the world for a long time I am content that others soon should occupy it. After all the point of a pattern is that it should be completed. When nothing can be added without spoiling the design the artist leaves it.

But now if anyone should ask me what is the use or sense of this pattern I should have to answer, none. It is merely something I have imposed on the senselessness of life because I am a novelist. For my own satisfaction, for my amusement and to gratify what feels to me like an organic need, I have shaped my life in accordance with a certain design, with a beginning, a middle and an end, as from people I have met here and there I have constructed a play, a novel or a short story. We are the product of our natures and our environment. I have not made the pattern I thought best, or even the pattern I should have liked to make, but merely that which seemed feasible. There are better patterns than mine. I do not believe that I am influenced only by an illusion natural to the man of letters to think that the best pattern of all is the husbandman's, who ploughs his land and reaps his crop, who enjoys his toil and enjoys his leisure, loves, marries, begets children and dies. When I have observed the peasantry in those favoured lands in which the earth produces her plenty without excessive labour, where the pleasures and pains of the individual are those incidental to the human race, it has seemed to me that there the perfect life was perfectly realized. There life, like a good story, pursues its way from beginning to end in a firm and unbroken line.

75

THE EGOISM of man makes him unwilling to accept the meaninglessness of life and when he has unhappily found himself no longer able to believe in a higher power whose ends he could flatter himself that he subserved he has sought to give it significance by constructing certain values beyond those that seem to further his immediate welfare. The wisdom of the ages has chosen three of these as most worthy. To aim at them for their own sake has seemed to give life some kind of sense. Though it can hardly be doubted that they too have a biologic utility, they have superficially an appearance of dis- interestedness which gives man the illusion that through them he escapes from human bondage. Their nobility strengthens his wavering sense of his spiritual significance and, whatever the result, the pursuit of them appears to justify his efforts. Oases in the vast desert of existence, since he knows no other end to his journey, man per- suades himself that they at all events are worth reaching and that there he will find rest and the answer to his question. These three values are Truth, Beauty and Goodness.

I have a notion that Truth finds a place in this list for rhetorical reasons. Man invests it with ethical qualities, such as courage, honour and independence of spirit, which indeed are often shown by his insistence on truth, but which in effect have nothing whatever to do with it. Finding in it so great an occasion for his own self-assertion he will be indifferent to any sacrifice that it entails. But then his interest is in himself and not in the truth. If truth is a value it is because it is true and not because it is brave to speak it. But truth is a character of judgements and so one would suppose that its value lay in the judgements it characterizes rather than in itself. A bridge that joined two great cities would be more important than a bridge that led from one barren field to another. And if truth is one of the ultimate values, it seems strange that no one seems quite to know what it is. Philosophers still quarrel about its meaning and the upholders of rival doctrines say many sarcastic things of one another. In these circumstances the plain man must leave them to it and content himself with the plain man's truth. This is a very modest affair and merely asserts something about particular existents. It is a bare statement of the facts. If this is a value one must admit that none is more neglected. The books on ethics give long lists of occasions on which it may be legitimately withheld; their authors might have saved themselves the trouble. The wisdom of the ages has long since decided that *toutes vérités ne sont pas bonnes á dire*. Man has always sacrificed truth to his vanity, comfort and advantage. He lives not by truth but by make-believe, and his idealism, it has sometimes seemed to me, is merely his effort to attach the prestige of truth to the fictions he has invented to satisfy his self-conceit.

76

BEAUTY STANDS in a better case. For many years I thought that it was beauty alone that gave significance to life and that the only purpose that could be assigned to the teeming generations that succeed one another on the face of the earth was to produce now and then an artist. The work of art, I decided, was the crowning product of human activity, and the final justification for all the misery, the endless toil and the frustrated strivings of humanity. So that Michelangelo might paint certain figures on the ceiling of the Sistine Chapel, so that Shakespeare might write certain speeches and Keats his odes, it seemed to me worth while that untold millions should have lived and suffered and died. And though I modified this extravagance later by including the beautiful life among the works of art that alone gave a meaning to life, it was still beauty that I valued. All these notions I have long since abandoned.

In the first place I discovered that beauty was a full stop. When I considered beautiful things I found that there was nothing for me to do but to gaze and admire. The emotion they gave me was exquisite, but I could not preserve it, nor could I indefinitely repeat it; the most beautiful things in the world finished by boring me. I noticed that I got a more lasting satisfaction from works of a more tentative character. Because they had not achieved complete success they gave more scope for the activity of my imagination. In the greatest of all works of art everything had been realized, I could give nothing, and my restless mind tired of passive contemplation. It seemed to me that beauty was like the summit of a mountain peak; when you had reached it there was nothing to do but to come down again. Perfection is a trifle dull. It is not the least of life's ironies that this, which we all aim at, is better not quite achieved.

I suppose that we mean by beauty that object, spiritual or material, more often material, which satisfies our æsthetic sense. That, however, tells you just about as much as you would know about water if you were told that it was wet. I have read a good many books to discover what the authorities had to say that made the matter a little plainer. I have known intimately a great many persons who were absorbed in the arts. I am afraid that neither from them nor from books have I learnt much that greatly profited me. One of the most curious things that has forced itself on my notice is that there is no permanence in the judgement of beauty. The museums are full of objects which the most cultivated taste of a period considered beautiful, but which seem to us now worthless; and in my own lifetime I have seen the beauty evaporate from poems and pictures, exquisite not so long ago, like hoar frost before the morning sun. Vain as we may be we can hardly think our own judgement ultimate; what we think beautiful will doubtless be scorned in another generation, and what we have despised may be raised to honour. The only conclusion is that beauty is relative to the needs of a particular generation, and that to examine the things we consider beautiful for qualities of absolute beauty is futile. If beauty is one of the values that give life significance it is something that is constantly changing and thus cannot be analysed, for we can as little feel the beauty our ancestors felt as we can smell the roses they smelt.

I have tried to find out from the writers on æsthetics what it is in human nature that makes it possible for us to get the emotion of beauty and what exactly this emotion is. It is usual enough to talk of the æsthetic instinct: the term seems to give it a place among the mainsprings of the human being, like hunger and sex, and at the same time to endow it with a specific quality that flatters the philosophic craving for unity. So æsthetics have been derived from an instinct of expression, an exuberance of vitality, a mystical sense of the absolute and I know not what. For my part I should have said it was not an instinct at all, but a state of the body-mind, founded in part on certain powerful instincts, but combined with human characteristics, which are the result of the evolutionary process, and with the common circumstances of life. That it has a great deal to do with the sexual instinct seems to be shown by the fact, commonly admitted, that those who possess an æsthetic sense of unusual delicacy diverge sexually from the norm to an extreme and often pathological degree. There may be in the constitution of the body-mind something that renders certain tones, certain rhythms and certain colours peculiarly attractive to man, so that there may be a physiological reason for the elements of what we consider beautiful. But we also find things beautiful because they remind us of objects, people or places, that we have loved or to which the passage of time has lent a sentimental value. We find things beautiful because we recognize them and contrariwise we find things beautiful because their novelty surprises us. All this means that association, by likeness or contrast, enters largely into the æsthetic emotion. It is only association that can explain the æsthetic value of the ugly. I do not know that anyone has studied the effect of time on the creation of beauty. It is not only that we grow to see the beauty of things as we know them better; it is rather that the delight that succeeding ages take in them somehow adds to their beauty. That, I suppose, is why certain works whose beauty now seems manifest should, when first given to the world, have attracted no great attention. I have a notion that the odes of Keats are more beautiful than when he wrote them. They are enriched by the emotion of all who have found solace and strength in their loveliness. Far then from thinking the æsthetic emotion a specific, simple affair, I think it is a very complicated one, which is made up of various, often discordant elements. It is no good for the æstheticians to say that you ought not to be moved by a picture or a symphony because it fills you with erotic excitement or melts you to tears by reminding you of some long-forgotten scene, or through its associations exalts you to mystic rapture. It does; and these sides of it are just as much part and parcel of the æsthetic emotion as the disinterested satisfaction in balance and composition.

What exactly is one's reaction to a great work of art? What does one feel when for instance one looks at Titian's Entombment in the Louvre or listens to the quintet in the Meistersinger? I know what mine is. It is an excitement that gives me a sense of exhilaration, intellectual but suffused with sensuality, a feeling of well-being in which I seem to discern a sense of power and of liberation from human ties; at the same time I feel in myself a tenderness which is rich with human sympathy;

I feel rested, at peace and yet spiritually aloof. Indeed on occasion, looking at certain pictures or statues, listening to certain music, I have had an emotion so strong that I could only describe it in the same words as those the mystics use to describe the union with God. That is why I have thought that this sense of communion with a larger reality is not only the privilege of the religious, but may be reached by other paths than prayer and fasting. But I have asked myself what was the use of this emotion. Of course it is delightful and pleasure in itself is good, but what is there in it that makes it superior to any other pleasure, so superior that to speak of it as pleasure at all seems to depreciate it? Was Jeremy Bentham so foolish after all when he said that one sort of happiness was as good as another, and if the amount of pleasure was equal pushpin as good as poetry? The answer the mystics gave to this question was unequivocal. They said that rapture was worthless unless it strengthened the character and rendered man more capable of right action. The value of it lay in works.

It has been my lot to live much among persons of æsthetic sensibility. I am not speaking now of the creators: to my mind there is a great difference between those who create art and those who enjoy it; the creators produce because of that urge within them that forces them to exteriorize their personality. It is an accident if what they produce has beauty; that is seldom their special aim. Their aim is to disembarrass their souls of the burdens that oppress them and they use the means, their pen, their paints or their clay, for which they have by nature a facility. I am speaking now of those to whom the contemplation and appreciation of art is the main business of life. I have found little to admire in them. They are vain and self-complacent. Inapt for the practical affairs of life, they disdain those who with humility perform the modest offices to which their destiny has constrained them. Because they have read a great many books or seen a great many pictures they think themselves superior to other men. They use art to escape the realities of life and in their imbecile contempt for common things deny value to the essential activities of humanity. They are no better really than drug-fiends; worse rather, for the drug-fiend at all events does not set himself on a pedestal from which to look down on his fellow-men. The value of art, like the value of the Mystic Way, lies in its effects. If it can only give pleasure, however spiritual that pleasure may be, it is of no great consequence or at least of no more consequence than a dozen oysters and a pint of Montrachet. If it is a solace, that is well enough; the world is full of inevitable evils and it is good that man should have some hermitage to which from time to time he may withdraw himself; but not to escape them, rather to gather fresh strength to face them. For art, if it is to be reckoned as one of the great values of life, must teach men humility, tolerance, wisdom and magnanimity. The value of art is not beauty, but right action.

If beauty is one of the great values of life, then it seems hard to believe that the æsthetic sense which enables men to appreciate it should be the privilege only of a class. It is not possible to maintain that a form of sensibility that is shared but by the elect can be a necessity of human life. Yet that is what the æsthetes claim. I must confess that in my foolish youth when I considered that art (in which I included the beauties of nature, for I was very much of opinion, as indeed I still am, that their beauty was constructed by men as definitely as they constructed pictures or symphonies) was the crown of human endeavour and the justification of man's existence, it gave me a peculiar satisfaction to think that it could be appreciated only by the chosen few. But this notion has long stuck in my gizzard. I cannot believe that beauty is the appanage of a set and I am inclined to think that a manifestation of art that has a meaning only to persons who have undergone a peculiar training is as inconsiderable as the set to which it appeals. An art is only great and significant if it is one that all may enjoy. The art of a clique is but a plaything. I do not know why distinctions are made between ancient art and modern art. There is nothing but art. Art is living. To attempt to give an object of art life by dwelling on its historical, cultural, or archæological associations is senseless. It does not matter whether a statue was hewn by an archaic Greek or a modern Frenchman. Its only importance is that it should give us here and now the æsthetic thrill and that this æsthetic thrill should move us to works. If it is to be anything more than a self-indulgence and an occasion for self-complacency, it must strengthen your character and make it more fitted for right action. And little as I like the deduction, I cannot but accept it; and this is that the work of art must be judged by its fruits, and if these are not good it is valueless. It is an odd fact, which must be accepted as in the nature of things and for which I know no explanation, that the artist achieves this effect only when he does not intend it. His sermon is most efficacious if he has no notion that he is preaching one. The bee produces wax for her own purposes and is unaware that man will put it to diverse uses.

77

IT APPEARS then impossible to say that either truth or beauty has intrinsic value. What about goodness? But before I speak of goodness I would speak of love; for there are philosophers who, thinking that it embraced every other, have accepted it as the highest of human values. Platonism and Christianity have combined to give it a mystical significance. The associations of the word lend it an emotion that makes it more exciting than plain goodness. Goodness in comparison is a trifle dull. But love has two meanings, love pure and simple, sexual love, namely; and loving-kindness. I do not think that even Plato distinguished them with exactness. He seems to me to ascribe the exultation, the sense of power, the feeling of heightened vitality which accompany sexual love to that other love which he calls the heavenly love and which I should prefer to call loving-kindness; and by doing so infects it with the ineradicable vice of earthly love. For love passes. Love dies. The great tragedy of life is not that men perish, but that they cease to love.

Not the least of the evils of life, and one for which there is small help, is that someone whom you love no longer loves you; when La Rochefoucauld discovered that between two lovers there is one who loves and one who lets himself be loved he put in an epigram the discord that must ever prevent men from achieving in love perfect happiness. However much people may resent the fact and however angrily deny it, there can surely be no doubt that love depends on certain secretions of the sexual glands. In the immense majority these do not continue indefinitely to be excited by the same object and with advancing years they atrophy. People are very hypocritical in this matter and will not face the truth. They so deceive themselves that they can accept it with complacency when their love dwindles into what they describe as a solid and enduring affection. As if affection had anything to do with love! Affection is created by habit, community of interests, convenience and the desire of companionship. It is a comfort rather than an exhilaration. We are creatures of change, change is the atmosphere we breathe, and is it likely that the strongest but one of all our instincts should be free from the law? We are not the same persons this year as last; nor are those we love. It is a happy chance if we, changing, continue to love a changed person. Mostly, different ourselves, we make a desperate, pathetic effort to love in a different person the person we once loved. It is only because the power of love when it seizes us seems so mighty that we persuade ourselves that it will last for ever. When it subsides we are ashamed, and, duped, blame ourselves for our weakness, whereas we should accept our change of heart as a natural effect of our humanity. The experience of mankind has led them to regard love with mingled feelings. They have been suspicious of it. They have as often cursed as praised it. The soul of man, struggling to be free, has except for brief moments looked upon the self-surrender that it claims as a fall from grace. The happiness it brings may be the greatest of which man is capable, but it is seldom, seldom unalloyed. It writes a story that generally has a sad ending. Many have resented its power and angrily prayed to be delivered from its burden. They have hugged their chains, but knowing they were chains hated them too. Love is not always blind and there are few things that cause greater wretchedness than to love with all your heart someone who you know is unworthy of love.

But loving-kindness is not coloured with that transitoriness which is the irremediable defect of love. It is true that it is not entirely devoid of the sexual element. It is like dancing; one dances for the pleasure of the rhythmic movement, and it is not necessary that one should wish to go to bed with one's partner; but it is a pleasant exercise only if to do so would not be disgusting. In loving-kindness the sexual instinct is sublimated, but it lends the emotion something of its own warm and vitalizing energy. Loving-kindness is the better part of goodness. It lends grace to the sterner qualities of which this consists and makes it a little less difficult to practise those minor virtues of self-control and self-restraint, patience, discipline and tolerance, which are the passive and not very exhilarating elements of goodness. Goodness is the only value that seems in this world of appearances to have any claim to be an end in itself. Virtue is its own reward. I am ashamed to have reached so commonplace a conclusion. With my instinct for effect I should have liked to end my book with some startling and paradoxical announcement or with a cynicism that my readers would have recognized with a chuckle as characteristic. It seems I have little more to say than can be read in any copybook or heard from any pulpit. I have gone a long way round to discover what everyone knew already.

I have little sense of reverence. There is a great deal too much of it in the world. It is claimed for many objects that do not deserve it. It is often no more than the conventional homage we pay to things in which we are not willing to take an active interest. The best homage we can pay to the great figures of the past, Dante, Titian, Shakespeare, Spinoza, is to treat them not with reverence, but with the familiarity we should exercise if they were our contemporaries. Thus we pay them the highest compliment we can; our familiarity acknowledges that they are alive for us. But when now and then I have come across real goodness I have found reverence rise naturally in my heart. It has not seemed to matter then that its rare possessors were perhaps sometimes a trifle less intelligent than I should have liked them to be. When I was a small boy and unhappy I used to dream night after night that my life at school was all a dream and that I should wake to find myself at home again with my mother. Her death was a wound that fifty years have not entirely healed. I have long ceased to have that dream; but I have never quite lost the sense that my living life was a mirage in which I did this and that because that was how it fell out, but which, even while I was playing my part in it, I could look at from a distance and know for the mirage it was. When I look back on my life, with its successes and its failures, its endless errors, its deceptions and its fulfilments, its joys and miseries, it seems to me strangely lacking in reality. It is shadowy and unsubstantial. It may be that my heart, having found rest nowhere, had some deep ancestral craving for God and immortality which my reason would have no truck with. In default of anything better it has seemed to me sometimes that I might pretend to myself that the goodness I have not so seldom after all come across in many of those I have encountered on my way had reality. It may be that in goodness we may see, not a reason for life nor an explanation of it, but an extenuation. In this indifferent universe, with its inevitable evils that surround us from the cradle to the grave, it may serve, not as a challenge or a reply, but as an affirmation of our own independence. It is the retort that humour makes to the tragic absurdity of fate. Unlike beauty, it can be perfect without being tedious, and, greater than love, time does not wither its delight. But goodness is shown in right action and who can tell in this meaningless world what right action is? It is not action that aims at happiness; it is a happy chance if happiness results. Plato, as we know, enjoined upon his wise man to abandon the serene life of contemplation for the turmoil of practical affairs and thereby set the claim of duty above the desire for happiness; and we have all of us, I suppose, on occasion adopted a course because we thought it right though we well knew that it could bring us happiness neither then nor in the future. What then is right action? For my own part the best answer I know is that given by Fray Luis de Leon. To follow it does not look so difficult that human weakness quails before it as beyond its strength. With it I can end my book. The beauty of life, he says, is nothing but this, that each should act in conformity with his nature and his business.

THE END

Elderberry was alone in the middle hall reading Air Marshal Beech's reminiscences. He, also, had lost his seat. His successful opponent, Gilpin, was not popular in the House but he was making his mark and had lately become an under-secretary. Elderberry had no habitation outside London. He had no occupation there. Most of his days and evenings were passed alone in this same armchair in Bellamy's.

He looked disapprovingly at Box-Bender's starched front.

"You still go out?"

"I had to give a party tonight for my daughter."

"Ah, something you had to pay for? That's different. It's being *asked* I like. I'm never asked anywhere now."

"I don't think you would have liked this party."

"No, no, of course not. But I used to get asked to dinners — embassies and that kind of thing. Well, so did you. There was a lot of rot talked but it did get one through the evening. Everything's very quiet here now."

This judgment was immediately rebutted by the descent of the Commando dinner party, who stumbled noisily down the staircase and into the billiard room.

Guy paused to greet his brother-in-law.

"I didn't ask you to our dance," said Box-Bender. "It is very small, for young people. I didn't suppose you'd want to come. Didn't know you ever came to London, as a matter of fact."

"I don't, Arthur. I'm just up to see lawyers. We've sold the Castello, you know."

"I'm glad to hear it. Who on earth can afford to buy property in Italy now? Americans, I suppose."

"Not at all. One of our countrymen who can't afford to live in England. Ludovic."

"Ludovic?"

"The author of *The Death Wish*. You must have heard of it."

"I think Angela read it. She said it was tosh."

"It sold nearly a million copies in America and they've just filmed it. He's a fellow I came across during the war. As a matter of fact the sale was arranged by a man who used to belong here — an American called Padfield. He seems to have become Ludovic's general factotum."

"Are they part of your party in there?"

"No. We aren't quite Ludovic's sort of party."

"Well, the Castello should be just the place for a literary man. How's everything at Broome?"

"Very well, thank you."

"Domenica all right, and the children?"

"Yes."

"Farm paying?"

"At the moment."

"Wish mine was. Well, give them all my regards." A voice called "Guy, come and play slosh."

"Coming, Bertie."

When he had gone, Elderberry said: "That's your brother-in-law, isn't it? He's putting on weight. Didn't I hear something rather sad about him during the war?"

"His wife was killed by a bomb."

"Yes, that was it. I remember now. But he's married again?"

"Yes. The first sensible thing he's ever done. Domenica Plessington, Eloise's girl. Eloise looked after the baby while

Guy was abroad. Domenica got very fond of it. A marriage was the obvious thing. I think Eloise deserves some credit in arranging it. No children of their own, but that's not always a disadvantage. Domenica manages the home farm at Broome. They've settled in the agent's house. They aren't at all badly off. Angela's Uncle Peregrine left his little bit to the child. Wasn't such a very little bit either."

Elderberry remembered that Box-Bender had had trouble with his own son. What had it been? Divorce? Debt? No, something odder than that. He'd gone into a monastery. With unusual delicacy Elderberry did not raise the question. He merely said: "So Guy's happily settled?"

"Yes," said Box-Bender, not without a small, clear note of resentment, "things have turned out very conveniently for Guy."